How to understand and improve
boys' learning

Mike Fleetham

Acknowledgements

I should like to thank my wife Lucy Fleetham and my mum Jill Bocquet for relieving me of my fatherly responsibilities temporarily while I wrote this book.

I am grateful to Chris Dickinson for inspiration, providing opportunities and ideas, and several rather good jokes.

Dedication

For men and boys – past, present and future:
Tommy Fleetham (1902–1993)
David Lloyd (1975–1993)
Brian Fleetham
Steve Bocquet
Arthur Fleetham
Sebastian Bocquet

The right of Mike Fleetham to be identified as the author of this work has been asserted by him in accordance with sections 77 and 78 of the Copyright, Designs and Patents Act 1988.

How to understand and improve boys' learning
MT10769
ISBN-13: 978 1 85503 432 7

© Mike Fleetham
Illustrations © Robin Edmonds
All rights reserved
First published 2008

Printed in the UK for LDA
Abbeygate House, East Road, Cambridge, CB1 1DB, UK

Contents

Contents

Introduction

How this book works

Section I: I Want to Understand Boys

In this section we shall look at what makes boys into boys, and think about the factors that influence their behaviour and learning. For example, did you know that four-day-old boys look at adult faces for only half the time that girls do? Did you know that it's likely that the majority of boys in a female teacher's classroom will be too warm to learn effectively?

Section II: I Want to Teach Boys Well

In this section we shall apply the knowledge gained from Section I, using it to enrich what you are doing well already, but with a greater focus on boys. You will discover how to play to boys' strengths and support their weaknesses, while still delivering the curriculum. We shall cover planning, classroom environment, teaching activities and professional development.

My contributors

It's likely that the majority of people who read this book will be female teachers. There is also a good possibility that a teacher's main point of contact with a child will be their mother. So, I thought it would be helpful to offer you three different perspectives to balance mine as a male teacher, father and consultant. At various points in the margins of this book three people will share their thoughts and ideas in order to add to the picture of boys and learning that is being created.

Why are boys perceived to be underachieving?

Let's explore this question by using a story.

> Lynne Williams is a senior primary-school teacher. Her thoughts about what I have written are in boxes like this. She will balance my male viewpoint with a practical, classroom-based female one.

> Jo Bourne is a parent of twin boys and an experienced primary-school teacher. In boxes like this are her thoughts on what I have written.

> Arthur is 8 years old, severely dyslexic and very intelligent. He likes *Star Wars*, golf, and finding things out. He hates reading and writing. The interesting things he has to say about what I've written are in boxes like this.

The tale of the Blidges and Gruffles

Several years ago in the land of Corticon, a distinguished and respected professor published a report that explored the significant and worsening underperformance of Blidges. Gruffles, on the other hand, were praised for their consistently high performance, which made the Blidges' lack of achievement even more apparent.

Corticon's supreme ruler was most concerned. The best magicians, warriors and healers were summoned and ordered to discover why Blidges performed so badly, and what could be done about it.

The magicians tried first. They cast spells, referred to ancient books, and looked for patterns of stars in the night sky. They concluded that the reason for the Blidges' underperformance was simply their lack of dedication and an aversion to hard work. They proposed that all Blidges should make more effort and work twice as many hours as Gruffles. But even when the Blidges' workload was doubled, they still underperformed.

Next the warriors had a turn. They set off on a quest, as warriors are prone to do. They believed that there was an evil creature that was impairing the Blidges' achievements. They searched the length, breadth and depth of Corticon to try to find it. After a significant number of days – probably 101, 366 or 7 – they found what they were seeking. The creature had a large, flat rectangular shape and its body was covered in flickering images. It had managed to infiltrate the minds of the Blidges and placed evil thoughts there. The warriors believed that if they slayed this beast, the Blidges would be free to excel. This the warriors did with relish, abandon and very sharp swords. However, the Blidges still remained far behind the Gruffles.

Finally the healers put their soft, warm hands on the heads of several Blidges. The healers closed their eyes, took several long and meaningful breaths and then shook their heads slowly. They said that Blidges could not be helped because they were destined to be underperformers from before their birth.

Corticon's supreme ruler became very angry. Why should Blidges play second fiddle to Gruffles? What was so special about Gruffles anyway? What did they do better than Blidges? It just wasn't right or fair.

Then, as the ruler pondered that final thought, the answer became obvious. You see, every year Blidges and Gruffles had their performance measured. Each one sat a test to monitor how good they were at patterwhacking. Now, everybody knows that Gruffles have always been good at patterwhacking, whereas Blidges don't enjoy it. Everyone also knows that Blidges are gifted at grubhuddling. However, there was no annual test for grubhuddling.

"I wish I knew about grubhuddling before."

Read the story again, but on this occasion substitute 'boys' for 'Blidges', 'girls' for 'Gruffles', 'writing' for 'patterwhacking' and 'building things' for 'grubhuddling'.

This story sums up my beliefs about boys' 'underachievement' in school. Boys, I believe, 'underperform' because they are generally better at things that don't have their performance measured. I'm not sure that there would be an issue if we measured the things boys excel at in ways that matched their strengths. If you measure a Blidge at patterwhacking, they underperform. If you measure a Blidge at grubhuddling, they excel. It's not rocket science, or frith minton as they say in Corticon.

I believe that we need to change the way we think about boys and their education. We need to enrich what we do to meet boys' needs, instead of seeking to 'solve the problem' of their 'underachievement'. There is a big gap, in my view, between boys' strengths and how we teach and assess them. I hope that the ideas in this book will help you to close that gap. As these ideas are all good teaching methods, I suggest that they will help girls too. By choosing to make yourself a better educator of boys, the girls you teach will benefit from your growth as well.

Section I:
I Want to Understand Boys

I visited Legoland® with my family recently. As I sat in one of the free-play areas, I made a note of the ways in which the boys and girls were behaving. The table that follows is a record of my observations.

What are the boys doing?	What are the girls doing?
Working alone	Working together
Building towers	Building houses and pyramids
Throwing Lego® bricks around	Talking quietly to each other
Shouting	Sharing Lego bricks
Moving between different work stations	Staying at the same workstation
Knocking over each other's constructions	Deciding who will live in their houses
Trying to build the tallest structure	Fending off boys

There are many factors at play in a boy's life and all of them influence his growth and learning. Some of these factors may be seen in the behaviour of the boys at Legoland. The main ones are as follows:

- ❍ Brain development – boys' brains grow differently from those of girls, and have developed over time to meet different needs. Brains need to be understood and looked after to get the most from them.

- ❍ Values – boys have unique ways of seeing themselves and the world in which they live. They may well value different things from their educators.

- ❍ Family – the adults, especially the men, and any children at home will each have a significant impact.

- ❍ School – a boy's belief about whether he is a successful person or not will be affected by the teaching and learning he experiences at school.

- ❍ Society – a boy's experiences outside school, including friends, extended family and the local community, will have an influence on his resilience.

- ❍ Culture – boys are bombarded with messages from the media, advertising and entertainment industries on a daily basis. They need careful guidance to help them to make sense of these powerful and sometimes dubious messages.

Boys have unique ways of seeing themselves and the world in which they live.

We shall look at each of these factors in a practical way so that we can build up a picture of what boys are like. From doing this, you will have a richer way of thinking about the boys you work with and a better idea of what you can do to support their learning. I hope you will become more able to see the world through a boy's eyes.

If you are intending to use these materials as part of a whole-school approach to understanding boys, you might like to do the following activity to help teachers and support staff get to grips with aspects of the six factors mentioned previously.

"Here's one we created earlier."

Build-a-boy

Audience
Teachers and support staff

Time
30–45 minutes, plus preparation

Learning outcome
To know that there are many factors that influence a boy's growth and learning

Organisation
Groups of 6

Resources
One build-a-boy template (see page 61), five split pins, and a pair of scissors for each group. A pen for each participant.

You can download an editable template of page 61 from www.thinkingclassroom.co.uk/boys

What to do
1. Give each group a copy of page 61 and five split pins, along with a pair of scissors and sufficient pens.
2. Each group chooses a boy whom they all know and who needs support.
3. One person per group cuts out the body parts on their worksheet and distributes them to the group, one each.
4. Each body part has a different question on it. A group member must answer it by writing a response on the relevant part. They may use the back if more space is needed.
5. Share responses in groups.
6. Each group assembles their boy using the split pins.
7. One person per group introduces their boy and shares their findings.

> **Lynne:** As teachers we have a responsibility to find out how our learners learn and why. It is well worth doing a little research on this. This may prevent a lot of headaches at the end of difficult days.

> **Jo:** The testosterone surge for a 4-year-old boy can be difficult when it coincides with starting school. If boys have a summer birthday, their bodies may be telling them to keep moving while some teachers may expect them to be quiet and still.

> **Arthur:** I shall tell my friends at school about being a girl when you are inside your mum.

Chapter 1
Boys' brains

Boys' and girls' brains are different in a number of ways, and much has been written about male thinking and behaviour as opposed to female. As neuroscience delves deeper into the brain and its workings, new explanations are suggested for these differences. We can use such findings to excuse what boys do, but it's more helpful to use them to guide our understanding of what boys need.

As with much of neuroscience, we need to beware of how we apply theories in case the use of labels limits our expectations of individuals. Differences in brain function from person to person may be slight, but not all boys may fit the norm. It would be unwise to build a school policy for teaching boys on neuroscience alone. However, there is much in neuroscience that can add to our understanding.

How boys' brains grow

What follows is a description of how a boy's healthy brain – let's use Arthur's – grows between the ages of 0 and 25.

What's happening	Implications
0: Conception	One more for the school roll in a few years.
24 hrs: Cell division begins.	
3 weeks: Arthur's neural tube forms and its cells divide rapidly to become neurons and glial cells. Glial cells help form a structure in which his neurons can sit. There are many more glial cells than neurons. Arthur's neural tube will eventually become his central nervous system.	Arthur will have a brain to learn with.
By the way, Arthur is female at this stage.	Arthur will be in the girls' line to go out to play.
8 weeks: Arthur's Y-chromosomes start up and the male hormone testosterone starts to be produced. This causes Arthur's penis and testicles to grow and stimulates subtle changes in his body and brain. Arthur is now male.	Arthur will be in the boys' line to go out to play.
8 weeks +: Arthur's genitals begin to produce even more testosterone. Over the next few months, it will make his brain: • grow more slowly than a baby girl's; • form fewer connections between his left and right hemispheres – his corpus callosum, which joins the two hemispheres, will be 25% smaller than a girl's; • develop a larger right hemisphere than a girl's – this is because when the right hemisphere sends out connections, the left isn't ready to receive them and so the connections grow in on themselves.	Arthur will learn more effectively when teachers respond to and respect the way his brain is working. Arthur will be better at some things than girls and slower to develop in other areas.

What's happening	Implications
2–3 months: Cells continue to divide and move to specific places within Arthur's growing central nervous system. Cells that end up in the wrong place may contribute to dyslexia, dyspraxia and autism.	Make sure a special needs policy is in place for dyslexia, dyspraxia and autism.
Arthur's brain hemispheres and spinal cord begin to form.	Arthur will be able to sit up straight in assembly.
15 weeks: Arthur's genitals are fully formed, though somewhat smaller than they will be at the age of 25.	Make sure a sex-education policy is in place.
4–5 months: Arthur's brain cells have reached their final destinations and have begun to send out axons and dendrites.	Make sure a thinking-skills policy is in place.
His synapses – the small gaps between one cell's axon and another's dendrite – begin to form.	
By 6 months: Arthur's brain will respond to voices and movements, and he will move his mouth as if he is singing in the womb.	Expose Arthur's mother to a wide variety of sounds, voices and music.
Birth: A 200 billion neuron learning machine is unleashed on the world, with as much testosterone in his bloodstream as in that of a 12-year-old boy. His brain makes 1 million new connections every second.	Every Child Matters begins.
4 days: Arthur spends approximately half the time that his sister did at the same age maintaining eye contact with adults.	Arthur may need support developing relationships with others.
2–3 months: Arthur's body has one-fifth of the testosterone level it had at birth.	
4 months: Arthur is less likely than a female baby of the same age to distinguish between a familiar adult and a stranger. He spends more time looking at objects moving in space than a girl of the same age does. She gives her attention to her care-giver's face and words.	Arthur may learn more effectively when movement is involved – his, an object or image's, or both.
9 months: Neural pruning begins. Arthur's excess of brain cells is rationalised, with the stronger connections remaining.	Early stimulation is essential.
2½–3 yrs: Arthur is aware that he is a boy.	Provide a variety of toys and experiences, such as dolls, swords, vacuum-cleaning, football, dressing-up, 2D and 3D art materials.
Arthur develops 'theory of mind' – the concept that he is an individual and other people have minds that think different things from his.	Brace yourself for tantrums and the forceful assertion of a brand-new, self-aware individual.
4 yrs: Arthur has a surge in testosterone.	Hang on to your hats and provide lots of activities to keep Arthur busy and engaged.
5 yrs: Arthur's testosterone levels drop by half.	Sit down and have a nice cup of tea.

What's happening	Implications
12 yrs: Arthur's testosterone levels begin to rise and brain cells begin to overproduce.	Parents renegotiate bedtime, phone allowance and bedroom noise level. Teachers, be aware that his brain is in turmoil.
13 yrs: The language areas in Arthur's brain are fully formed.	Keep Arthur exposed to language and languages throughout his primary-school years. It's not too late at secondary, but it's a whole lot harder.
14 yrs: Arthur's testosterone levels peak at 800% of his toddler levels, causing all sorts of fun and games for teachers, parents and girlfriends.	Parents spend long evenings drinking wine and discussing teenagers with other parents. Teachers need to form good relationships with him and channel his energy into learning.
25 yrs: Arthur's testosterone levels are maintained, but his body is used to them and his life experience is able to cope with them.	Sit back and be proud of a man well made.

At the beginning of Section II, we shall discover more about the unique boy brain, and work out how to cater for it in the classroom. For now, have a look at the list of behaviours that follows:

1. taking risks
2. doing one thing at a time
3. expressing emotions
4. spotting patterns
5. doing several things at once
6. playing co-operatively
7. moving around a lot
8. playing football
9. building things
10. charming an adult
11. climbing trees
12. listening well.

Draw and number a horizontal scale like the one shown for each statement in the list. Label them with a male symbol at one end and a female symbol at the other. Put a cross along each scale to indicate how much the related statement is a boy trait. For example, you might place 'expressing emotions' three-quarters of the way towards the female symbol because you believe that girls are generally better at this than boys, although boys do have some ability in this area.

It will be interesting to try this activity again at the end of reading the book to see if your views have changed, and in what ways.

How to care for boys' brains

Boys' brains, like all brains, need looking after if they are to work properly. Diet, rest, exercise and stimulation all play a part.

Diet

To find out more on this subject, try these.
www.fi.edu/brain/pyramid.html
Dump the Junk by Mary Whiting
The Food our Children Eat by Joanna Blythman
Details of books mentioned are on page 60.

A balanced diet should include the following five food groups.

- bread, cereals and potatoes (carbohydrate): about one-third
- fruit and vegetables (vitamins, minerals, fibre): about one-third
- meat, fish, eggs, beans, nuts and pulses (protein): about one-sixth
- dairy products (calcium and protein): about one-sixth
- foods high in fats and sugar (junk food, sweets and cakes – all the stuff you crave after a tough day with Year 6): no more than one-twelfth

Fluid is important too, a good daily intake being six to eight drinks, preferably not sugary ones.

Rest

"It's a blood flow thing."

Neurologist Ruben Gur believes that the male brain is programmed to recharge itself between tasks, which it does by entering a rest state. This might explain why boys drift off during lessons. Brain scans have shown that this rest state is essential to male brain function. Apparently it's linked to blood flow in the brain. There are many reasons why some boys don't get enough sleep – late nights, early starts, TV or computer consoles in their bedrooms, and so on. It's important to do what we can to give our boys' brains the rest they need. There are some practical suggestions to help with this in Section II.

Exercise

In 2002, the British Heart Foundation and the Health Education Authority expressed concerns about the increasing number of obese children in our schools. They recommended that each child should have an hour of moderate exercise each day – walking, swimming, dancing, cycling – and a couple of sessions aimed at increasing muscular strength, flexibility and bone health each week – climbing, skipping, jumping, gymnastics. Exercise increases oxygen uptake by the brain, and several studies have linked regular exercise to increased academic performance.

Stimulation

Different parts of a boy's brain are responsible for different functions. For example, the area in the left hemisphere just above the ear plays a major role in language creation. The equivalent part on the right looks after aspects of musical ability. The area at the front behind the forehead manages high-order thinking, gives a boy a sense of who he is and allows him to self-regulate – to think before acting.

Many other areas across and within the brain contribute to a boy's potential to succeed in any field of human endeavour. Therefore it's important to stimulate as much of his brain as possible so that he can discover exactly what he's good at and what he wants to do in life. These long-term goals will also bring short-term benefits as the stimulation involved will help him to learn and recall information more effectively. The more of a boy's brain that has been stimulated by an experience, the more chance he has of remembering it.

In the classroom we can stimulate a boy's brain by providing an exciting variety of challenges, sensations, activities and experiences.

In the classroom we can stimulate a boy's brain by providing an exciting variety of challenges, sensations, activities and experiences – something that early years' teachers often do naturally. Sadly, this rich diet may become less so as boys grow older and are required to take tests. However, their brains don't suddenly rewire in Year 2 or 3 and say, 'Please, no more active learning, I'm ready to sit still and listen now.' There are details on how to upgrade your learning menu for boys in Section II.

It's not only the variety of stimuli that is important; so is the frequency and consistency of it. When a pathway in the brain is fired up repeatedly, more myelin coating is laid down. This makes the pathway much more effective as the signals travelling along it are stronger and quicker. It's like cutting a pathway through the jungle. It's difficult the first time because a route needs to be created. Once the clearing has been done, it is much easier and quicker to take the path. Yet if you don't walk along the path for a while, the jungle will begin to grow back and eventually block the way.

Special brains

Dyslexia

Dyslexia is a difficulty in processing language, especially when reading. The majority of learners diagnosed with it are boys. However, it's likely that many dyslexic girls go unnoticed because they respond to the challenges presented by their difficulties in different ways from boys. Boys generally use the left hemisphere of their brain only in language tasks, whereas girls use both sides. This means that girls have extra resources to bring to bear on their difficulties. Both my children are dyslexic. My daughter hid her problems well until Year 5. My son, thankfully, was less able to do so and was identified in Year 3. The British Dyslexia Association estimates that 10 per cent of learners are dyslexic, with 4 per cent being severely affected. In 70 per cent of cases a genetic link can be established, usually on the male side of the family.

Dyslexics are often labelled for their language difficulties, rather than valued for their strengths in other areas. If you have a dyslexic boy in your class, it's important to discover, value and use his strengths, not just meet his language needs. He may have hidden these very well after years of perceived failure and a focus on what he can't do. A dyslexic brain is often skilled with images – visualisation, imagination, creativity. Look out for these and encourage them.

A dyslexic brain is different from a non-dyslexic one in several ways. Research by P.E. Simos and others identified one striking difference when it comes to reading. In dyslexics and non-dyslexics alike, one part of the brain – the left basal temporal cortex – fires up within 200 milliseconds of exposure to text. Then, within 600 milliseconds, the language areas on the left side of the non-dyslexic's brain wake up and start processing words. However, the dyslexic brain doesn't do this. Instead of the language areas on the left firing up, the equivalent areas on the right side of the brain do so.

For more on this project, visit www.scilearn.com

For further reading:
How to Identify and Support Children with Dyslexia by Chris Neanon

Dyslexia can't be cured, but there are many interventions that can help. E. Temple and others investigated Fast ForWord language software and discovered that regular use over an eight-week period can reactivate the left side of the dyslexic brain and lead to improved reading ability. The dyslexic children in the study were still slower than normal readers – 800 milliseconds to activate the language areas rather than 600 milliseconds – but improvements like this provide hope for the many boys who face a daily struggle with words in the classroom.

Dyspraxia

Dyspraxia is a brain-based difficulty with voluntary movement. It's estimated that 6 per cent of learners are dyspraxic to a level where help is needed, and 80 per cent of these children are boys. A dyspraxic learner may be clumsy and forgetful, move awkwardly and have language difficulties. They may struggle to work and learn with other children and not understand important social rules, such as turn-taking and group hierarchy. This can lead to exclusion from friendship groups and a loss of self-esteem. It's easy to label these children as disruptive or annoying – I've been guilty of this – and make them miss a few playtimes, but they can't help their behaviour. They are wired that way.

To find out more visit www.dyspraxiafoundation.org.uk.

For further reading:
Developmental Dyspraxia: Identification and Intervention by Madeleine Portwood
How to Understand and Support Children with Dyspraxia by Lois Addy

Like dyslexia, dyspraxia is believed to be caused by incorrect cell migration as the brain and central nervous system form. The problem seems to be to do with the cerebellum, located at the back of the brain, and the left and right hemispheres, which seem to fail to communicate effectively.

Dyspraxia can't be cured, but many steps can be taken to improve the life and learning of those with it. These include exercise routines, language support and behaviour modification programmes.

Autism Spectrum Disorder (ASD)

Learners with autism may have difficulty with social interaction and communication. They may have a narrow range of interests which they are often obsessive about, and limited imagination. The autism spectrum ranges from profound disability to milder forms, such as Asperger's syndrome. It is believed that 80 per cent of learners with ASD are boys.

The autistic brain has five major differences compared to a normal one. These and their main consequences are as follows:

- ● the frontal lobes are larger – reasoning is impaired
- ● the corpus callosum is smaller – co-ordination across the brain is impaired
- ● the amygdala is larger – threats are registered where they don't exist
- ● the hippocampus is larger – more social situations have to be remembered
- ● the cerebellum is larger – physical co-ordination is impaired.

Dr Simon Baron-Cohen argues that the autistic brain is the ultimate male brain. Extreme forms of autism require expert help, and these learners are often best served by specialist schools.

The James Brindley School in Birmingham, England, is a world leader in its work with children for whom mainstream schools are unsuitable, and these include children with ASD. I am privileged to work there regularly and with each visit I learn a little more about autism. Over this time I've worked with a boy who will use only blue paper, one who believes he is a car, and another who knows intimately all 251 levels of the Pac-Man game. I've come to realise that, as far as these people are concerned, that's normal behaviour – and who are we to say otherwise?

Attention Deficit Disorder and Attention Deficit Hyperactivity Disorder

Attention Deficit Disorder (ADD) and Attention Deficit Hyperactivity Disorder (ADHD) are often regarded as developmental difficulties. This means that they will appear after birth, usually between the ages of 3 and 5 years, rather than being in place prenatally. Those that favour this view argue that poor diet, inadequate parenting and exposure to toxins are the reasons for these disorders. Other experts believe that both disorders are genetic and caused by the brain struggling to make the neurotransmitter dopamine.

Children with these disorders may be inattentive, hyperactive and impulsive. Typical characteristics include:

- ● making careless mistakes in school work
- ● difficulty in keeping on task
- ● squirming in seat
- ● not listening when spoken to directly
- ● not following instructions

- ● avoiding things that take a lot of mental effort over a sustained period of time
- ● easily distracted
- ● fidgeting with hands or feet
- ● getting up from seat
- ● interrupting others.

Find out more:
National Autistic Society:
www.nas.org.uk

James Brindley School:
www.jamesbrindley.bham.
sch.uk

For further reading:
Asperger's Syndrome: A Guide for Parents and Professionals by Tony Attwood
How to Support and Teach Children on the Autism Spectrum by Dave Sherratt
The Curious Incident of the Dog in the Night Time by Mark Haddon

Boys with these conditions outnumber girls by three to one. You may well be thinking that these characteristics just describe boys in general. You would be right; most boys will exhibit some or all of these behaviours from time to time. However, with children with ASD or ADHD these characteristics will be constant.

One of the recent responses to ADHD is to prescribe a stimulant, such as Ritalin. This drug stimulates the areas of the brain responsible for focus, attention and impulse control. However, there is much debate about whether young children should be given such a powerful chemical. Non-chemical responses are available, although some of the latest research suggests that medical interventions are more effective than behaviour modification.

The author Steve Biddulph goes so far as to propose that a lot of ADD cases are instances of DDD – Dad Deficit Disorder. He believes that many of the poor behaviours characteristic of boys with ADHD can be improved by enriching the father–son relationship. There is more about this on pages 19–20.

Cave boys

Evolutionary psychology combines evolutionary theory with brain development to investigate how natural selection has shaped our brains over thousands of years into the ones we use today to shop, watch TV, write lesson plans and sell stuff on eBay. It can be very interesting. No, really, it can. What's fascinating is how behaviours of the twenty-first century may be traced back to our cave-dwelling ancestors. As a final view on boys' brains, consider the following:

● When a boy is being fussy about what he eats, it may be because he's hard wired by nature to be picky. Scientists have suggested that young children turn their noses up at vegetables and strange meats because evolution has taught them to watch out for poisonous plants.

● When a boy focuses intently on one thing and ignores what's going on around him, it could be courtesy of his ancestors. Males developed a long, narrow field of vision to help on their hunting expeditions, while the females, with a wider field of vision, stayed in the caves protecting the children or gathered nuts and berries nearby. This behaviour itself has passed down the centuries to today's shopping habits. Women I know have commented that they select their garment but instead of buying it hide it on a different rail, coming back later to retrieve it and make their purchase, in case they find something better elsewhere. This shrewd behaviour can perhaps be traced back to finding a cache of berries, hiding it under a pile of leaves and continuing on to seek better pickings.

● Boys are acutely aware of the hierarchies and pecking order within a class. They learn about allegiances, pacts and collaboration quickly, which can perhaps be traced back to ancient tribal organisation.

Having taken some valuable time to look at boys' brains, we shall now move on and explore the second key factor that influences their lives and learning.

Chapter 2
Boys' values

The words we use reveal our beliefs, which in turn are manifestations of our values. Take the following example: 'I can't do it. I'll never be able to. School's crap. You're always telling me what to do.' I'm sure we've all experienced words to this effect in our teaching careers. Let's take these words and look at the beliefs being expressed through them.

Words	Beliefs
I can't do it. I'll never be able to.	I have fixed and inadequate abilities.
School's crap.	My needs are more important than school.
You're always telling me what to do.	I'm more important than you.

On the other hand, we might hear, or might prefer to hear, the following: 'At last, I can do it. School's great. We're working well together.'

Words	Beliefs
At last, I can do it.	I have abilities that will grow to meet challenges.
School's great.	My needs are compatible with school.
We're working well together.	We're all important.

How human values change

A deeper understanding of boys comes with an appreciation of what they value and how this changes over time.

A deeper understanding of boys comes with an appreciation of what they value and how this changes over time. Spiral Dynamics (SDi) is an excellent model for thinking about this. The theory was devised by Clare Graves and developed by Don Beck and Chris Cowan, and then further by Ken Wilber. Put simply, SDi proposes that a person's values change and grow upwards through a series of levels during their lifetime. At each stage different things are viewed as important and valuable. People at the same level will see the world in a similar way and be able to live and work together. However, people who are not at the same level may disagree with each other as they place significance on different things.

The SDi model is based on a spiral that symbolises connected growth, with each stage assigned a different colour. The different levels are shown in the summary that follows.

Level	Colour	Motivation	What's valued
Survival	Beige	Survival	Food, shelter and sex
Tribal	Purple	Belonging	Acceptance by the group
Empire	Red	Being in charge	I and my needs
Authority	Blue	Following rules	The system and its rules
Strategic	Orange	Collaborating for success	We and our success
Social	Green	Valuing everyone equally	Human diversity
Systemic	Yellow	Seeking the bigger picture	Integration of different world views

As people get older, they move up through the levels. Sometimes they get stuck for a time before moving on, and not everyone will make it through all stages. It's important to know that each new stage includes elements of what has already been worked through. So someone at green (Social) can and will be orange (Strategic) from time to time. According to SDi theory, only those who have reached yellow (Systemic) fully accept the existence of all the other levels. Let's use this powerful idea to think about working with boys in school.

What boys value

The beige level (Survival) is associated with survival needs at birth, though some severely neglected boys will present the behaviours of this level at school. A starving and abused boy will seek food and acceptance. Purple (Tribal) is associated with the magical beliefs of childhood and red (Empire) with toddler-style tantrums. Blue (Authority) expresses how a boy is required to conform to school, social and religious systems; whereas orange (Strategic) and green (Social) represent his emerging teenage self. Yellow (Systemic) is reached, if at all, in the adult years. As a boy moves through the different stages, his values will evolve. At each stage he will discover the opportunity for positive and negative behaviour. Here's how this might look in school for the five levels you're most likely to encounter.

Colour	Positive behaviour in school	Negative behaviour in school
Purple	• Is part of the class and a member of the school community. • Expresses the awe and wonder of childhood.	• Rejects those who do not seem to fit. • Blindly follows powerful/charismatic boys without thinking for himself.
Red	• Leads other children well. • Meets his targets for improvement. • Puts his needs before those of other children.	• Bosses, bullies and devalues other children.

Colour	Positive behaviour in school	Negative behaviour in school
Blue	• Follows the rules. • Does as he's told in anticipation of a reward.	• Unable to learn independently. • Unable to be creative and think outside the box.
Orange	• Collaborates well with other children. • Values team competition.	• Unable to accept coming second. • Sees everything as a competition.
Green	• Accepts and values other children. • Puts his needs on a level with those of other children.	• May be too tolerant and devalue himself. • Unable to make a decision if someone is going to lose out.

What teachers value

Now, let's take a look at the teachers working with these boys. They will have a value system too, but there's a very good chance that it will be different from that of the children they teach. However hard this may be, it's our responsibility as adults to accept where boys are coming from and meet them at that point. A 'blue' teacher in front of 'red' boys needs to appreciate where they are and respond accordingly. A 'green' teacher inheriting a class of 'blue' boys needs to start from the rules they value and then gently move them on.

SDi provides not only a description of different values, but activities for moving people on to the next level. For example, a boy functioning at orange (Strategic) will, with guidance, move to green (Social) when he realises that there is more to life than winning. It can be very comfortable staying at one level – and many people do this for their whole life – but growth, learning and evolving values bring greater rewards in the end.

I wanna be the leader!

I think he's at the red stage today.

Colour	Positive teacher behaviour	Negative teacher behaviour
Purple	• Is part of the class and a member of the school community. • Brings a touch of magic to learning.	• Rejects those who do not seem to to fit. • Blindly follows powerful/charismatic colleagues without thinking for themselves.
Red	• Demonstrates self-confidence. • Meets their performance targets.	• Arrogant, bossy, shows off. • Puts their needs before the children's.
Blue	• Follows the rules. • Does as they are told in anticipation of a reward.	• Unable to respond realistically to new initiatives. • Unable to be creative and think outside the box.
Orange	• Collaborates well with colleagues. • Values team competition.	• Unable to accept coming second. • Sees everything as a competition.
Green	• Accepts and values everyone in the school community. • Puts their needs on a level with everyone else's.	• May be too tolerant and devalue themselves. • Unable to make a decision if someone is going to lose out.

Chapter 3
Boys and their families

Boys spend most of their time with their families and will be shaped by the relationships that are built there. However, family structures and work patterns are not what they were, and this has put boys at risk. A boy may experience transient and turbulent relationships as a result of his parents separating and seeking new partners. He may need to relearn his place in the family as step-brothers and step-sisters arrive, or as he moves between two or more different houses. With greater work mobility, parents may spend a great deal of time away from home, arriving back either too late or too tired, or both, for any meaningful interaction with their sons. All in all, a boy has a harder time getting what he needs than he would have done forty years ago.

A boy has a harder time getting what he needs than he would have done forty years ago.

Family expectations

Professor Carol Dweck, professor of psychology at Columbia University, is an expert on motivation, personality and development. Her research has produced a fascinating and immensely important finding regarding how people view themselves and what they expect of others. Her Self Theory places people along a continuum that begins with 'Incrementalist' at one extreme and finishes with 'Entitist' at the other.

Incrementalists believe that their efforts will make a difference, that problems can be overcome and that learning, however difficult, will pay off. Entitists, on the other hand, believe they can do little to improve their lot. Problems and difficulties are simply confirmation of their own biological limitations. What is significant in terms of boys and their families is that children have already decided what they believe about themselves by the age of 3 years, and this is largely due to parental expectations.

In his book *Father to the Man*, Christopher Hallowell shares a personal anecdote that shows how powerful parental expectation can be. His father attempts to teach him how to build a wooden box, but insists that it must be square. Hallowell eventually produces a rickety, skewed affair, whereupon his father scowls and says, 'You didn't get something square. You will never be a good builder unless you can get something square.' Hallowell kept the box for storing odds and ends, but each time he lifted the lid, he saw his father's scowling face.

Dads and lads

As I write this section of the book, I'm looking out of a window at my parents' garden. My father is mowing the lawn and my son is helping by pushing him along with his hands on his lower back, and emptying the grass box from time to time. As I do this, I know I'm about to advise you to encourage fathers to spend time with their sons. As a working dad who is frequently away from home, and writing books when he returns, I'm all too aware of the practical issues and emotional strength needed to give a son what he needs.

R.W. Blanchard and H.B. Biller studied the effect of the father and son relationship on academic performance with third-grade – Year-4 – boys. They looked at families where dads were absent and ones where they were present. They categorised the 'present' fathers as either 'available' or 'unavailable'. As I type this, I am present yet unavailable to my son. Blanchard and Biller discovered that boys with absent fathers performed the worst at school, and those with present and available fathers did the best. Those with unavailable dads fell somewhere in between.

Boys tend to be more reliant on their mother or female carer for their first five or six years of their lives. However, at about 7 years they will begin to move away from her and seek out their father or male carer. They want to learn how to be men and their dad is the first port of call. It's desirable, though sadly not always practical, that their dads or male carers are available to give boys what they need. Dads are now seen as a valuable resource to boost boys' engagement with learning. There are a lot of national projects and initiatives to help them to spend time together. Many of these focus on reading and use football as a hook. Others create space and time for fathers and sons to be together on adventure weekends. Getting dads into school to share their skills, experience and maleness will be well worth the effort.

Find out more:
www.literacytrust.org.uk/
Campaign/menandboys.html

Michael Gurian, in his inspirational book *The Minds of Boys*, suggests an innovative solution to the problem of getting families to support boys' learning. Rather than bemoaning the loss of traditional extended-family structures, he wisely suggests that we work with what we have and create parent-led learning teams for boys. These loose and flexible teams would comprise any trusted adults in the boy's life who have something unique to offer them. It may be that Grandma can teach him to sew on buttons, helping him to develop an important life skill and fine-motor proficiency. A friend's father may know about computers and be prepared to coach him through the basics of word-processing. A neighbour may be willing to spend time reading with him in return for his doing a few chores for them. What Gurian suggests is a twenty-first century interpretation of the way ancient tribes probably educated their young ones, and it serves as a powerful ally to school learning.

Chapter 4
Boys and their schools

Assessment

School phases start and/or end with a test. Whether it's the Foundation Stage Profile, SATs or GCSEs, the data indicate that boys consistently underperform when compared to girls. It is true to say that there are examples of the pattern beginning to be reversed. Boys do start to catch up at A-level, nearly matching girls at physics and significantly narrowing the gap in English. However, it's sobering to know that, according to the Leverhulme Primary Improvement Project run by Exeter University, boys' reading ability is consistently 4–5 per cent behind girls' throughout their primary-school years.

As I've said earlier, if we were to change what we assess and the way we assess it, then the boys might well outperform the girls. At present we're working in a system that favours girls, so we shall have to work with that and do the best that we can for the boys.

I recently set up a poll on my website to investigate this issue informally. I asked people to vote about whether they thought that current assessment methods favour girls, boys, neither or both. The ninety-seven people who responded did so in the following ways:

- Girls – 6%
- Boys – 49%
- Neither – 35%
- Both – 10%

The impact of school

A boy's experience of school will either turn him on to learning or switch him off completely. The following factors will all influence his learning behaviour:

- the way lessons are structured
- the support he is given
- the praise he is given
- the rules he works and learns under
- the value placed on his achievements
- the way his transgressions are dealt with
- the resources available to him
- how comfortable he feels
- how much freedom he is given
- the variety of learning styles catered for
- the number of chances per day he is given to succeed
- his quality of his relationships with his teachers
- the quality of his relationships with his friends and classmates
- the subjects on offer for study
- the quality of his playtimes
- the opportunity he has to be himself.

Section II is dedicated to helping you make boys' experiences in school ones that they value and want to engage with.

Lynne: One of the hardest things is having to administer tests. After working hard to build self-esteem and cater for learning styles, you have to watch them be destroyed almost. One test might unravel everything because it doesn't allow boys to show their best.

Jo: My sons have little or no contact with men during their school day. They have a loving hands-on dad who can guide them towards manhood, but some boys in their school do not have this. Perhaps schools could invite men into the classroom.

Arthur: Doing a test is hard and annoying because there are all sorts of things to do and there are too many and your brain gets really tired. Especially with a reading test.

Do you think this is a girls' test?

I'll write a report summarising my views for you.

Chapter 5
Boys and society

As boys reach their teenage years, they will begin to move away from their mother and father and seek alternative male company. This behaviour appears in many ancient cultures, including that of Native Americans. In such cultures as theirs, teenage boys enter the forest to watch the men and learn from them. At some point they will go through an initiation experience, often a lone journey during which they must complete a difficult task.

Boys still need the guidance of men today – perhaps even an initiation experience and a task by which to prove their worth. However, opportunities to do these things are less abundant now and can be dangerous. Boys seeking to become men in society often find themselves doing so in the wrong way and with the wrong people, as the following examples show:

- In 2004, D.P. Farrington and K. Painter looked at the risk factors for criminal offending in families. They found that convictions for offences were much higher for brothers (44%) than for sisters (12%), offending males choosing burglary and vehicle theft and females shoplifting and deception.
- Between 1999 and 2005 9,853 Anti-Social Behaviour Orders (ASBOs) were issued in England and Wales. An ASBO may be issued to anyone aged 10 years or above who has acted in an anti-social manner. Although no official figures are held for the gender split, a source in the Crown Prosecution Service has indicated to me that up to 92 per cent of these ASBOs were issued to males.
- In 2006 the UK prison population was 73,965 males and 4,478 females.

All too often boys are drawn to unsuitable companions and immature belief systems in the absence of genuine and valuable ones. This is why it's important for society to provide trusted males and safe activities for the next generation of men. These activities could include:

- swimming lessons
- tennis lessons
- golf lessons
- Beavers, Cubs and Scouts
- cadets
- time with trusted male family friends or relatives
- part-time job
- helping someone who is retired
- community service
- joining a football team.

An excellent example of providing for boys to learn effectively in society was initiated in 2001 to coincide with the release of the first *Lord of the Rings* film. The Lord of the Rings in Libraries project was a partnership between four organisations:

- the National Reading Campaign
- Collins Children's Books
- Games Workshop plc
- the Chartered Institute of Library and Information Professionals (CILIP).

Public and school libraries hosted workshops based on the *Lord of the Rings*, which attracted many boys and young men who would otherwise not have thought to go into a library. In 2005 Games Workshop built on the project's success by developing a network of clubs in libraries across the country. They provided a dedicated team to help librarians set up and maintain the clubs.

If you have a Games Workshop nearby, step inside one Saturday morning and take a look. You will see boys and men engaged in purposeful activity, whether they are building and creating fantasy models or playing the strategic games of Warhammer or Warhammer 40,000. Look even closer and you will see a great deal of the National Curriculum covered by midday.

Boys and culture

In this age of video games and mobile phones, there must still be a place for knots, tree-houses and stories of incredible courage.

Con and Hal Iggulden,
The Dangerous Book
for Boys

One of the most powerful yet subtle influences on a boy is the culture in which he lives. He is exposed to messages about who he should be, what he should think and how he should behave on a daily basis. Some of these messages come implicitly from the adults around him and others are beamed at him through television, the Internet and computer games. In the face of such potent signals, we need to draw boys' attention to their more positive features and help them think through what culture is trying to tell them.

Heroes and role models

Boys are exposed to hundreds of different male characters and will identify quickly with certain ones. Boys need someone to copy, someone to show them how to grow up and to indicate what they might become. Father figures, older brothers and family friends may take this role, but fiction and celebrity provide attractive, exciting and often rebellious role models – Bart Simpson, Harry Potter, David Beckham and others all have an allure for boys.

In a recent TV show the presenter Richard Hammond went on a quest for the ultimate boys' fiction book. In interviewing young readers and children's authors, he explored the sort of hero boys most want to read about.

Such characters were likely to be:

- ❍ slightly older than the reader
- ❍ a little bit anti-authority
- ❍ male
- ❍ based in a place and time that the reader could identify with
- ❍ believable.

These heroes needed to be placed in a story that:

- ❍ was full of action
- ❍ used machines and gadgets
- ❍ included details, facts and data
- ❍ had a constantly unfolding plot and a twist at the end
- ❍ included humour
- ❍ involved magic and alternative worlds.

Lynne: Don't ignore boys' interests and heroes. Use them. I found myself discovering facts about football players that I was able to bring into learning activities, using them as a basis for a scenario or a problem to solve.

Jo: I let my sons watch television – there is a place for this medium. They are attracted to the cartoon *Horrid Henry*. As long as parents explain that this is not the sort of behaviour and language expected or tolerated at school, then teachers can heave a sigh of relief.

Arthur: TV is interesting and nice. If you're bored you can turn it on. I like the Cartoon Network. I think people like TV because you don't have to do anything.

What boys see
Television and computer games

Each year, a boy spends up to 190 days in school and around five hours of each day in lessons. If he spends three hours a day watching TV, he experiences more TV hours than learning ones (1,095 versus 950). Michael Gurian states that the average American child spends 900 hours a year in school and 1,023 watching TV. The two sets of figures are remarkably similar.

I recently looked through our lounge window and saw my own children in front of the TV. They didn't realise I was there, even though I wasn't particularly well hidden. They were captivated and fully engaged with the latest show on the Cartoon Network. I imagined freezing the scene, removing the TV and taking a closer look at their faces. I think I would have seen two blank expressions fixed on a point ahead of them, each giving the impression of someone who is daydreaming, suffering a petit mal seizure or has been charmed by the White Witch. However, as I continued to watch they did respond by laughing at a funny part of the show and shifting position on the sofa. On page 62 is a quick test to see how clued up you are on children's TV shows.

Dimitri Christakis is a researcher at a children's hospital in Seattle who is passionately concerned about the detrimental influence that he believes television has on young children. He argues that a child's brain needs a rich variety of sensory stimulation in order to grow fully. For a young boy this includes the vital experience of being active. Watching television can restrict this variety of stimulation severely.

In his research Christakis claims that 'for every hour of television watched per day, the incidence of ADD and ADHD increases by 10%'. His basis for this statement is the findings from tests on a sample of 2,600 children, whom he monitored from birth to 7 years old. He noticed that there were 10 per cent more cases of children with ADD or ADHD in the group of children who watched television for two hours a day than in the group that watched one hour a day.

We have to be careful with findings like these because the results may not be causal. There is no proof that television is causing ADD or ADHD, only an observation that children with ADD or ADHD appear to watch more television than other children.

To balance this view, Stuart Biddle, professor of exercise and sport psychology at Loughborough University, published research in 2007 that claimed that children who watch television are not 'couch potatoes'. He asked over 1,500 12- to 16-year-olds to keep detailed diaries of what they did every fifteen minutes outside school hours. He concluded through studying these accounts that those children who watched a lot of television were actually as active as those who watched less.

"Watch me – you know you want to."

Find out more:
http://uk.wii.com

Generally, boys need to move to learn, and their brains need to be active to grow properly. Television and computer games can inhibit this because they often provide a diet of quickly changing sounds and images that keep viewers passively in one place. Television can be alluring to a boy's brain as he can select programmes that don't require him to engage actively with the material, or put any effort into lengthy periods of concentration. No wonder we have our work cut out to make our lessons stimulating and keep boys' interest. Television is a hard act to follow, especially as Sky TV currently offers twenty-four different children's channels.

I hope this section hasn't depressed you. Although television and computer games are not going to disappear, it doesn't have to be all bad news. We, as educators, have a role to play. This is to manage the use of television and computer games, and to model appropriate and regulated viewing to the boys we work with. There are some educational and entertaining programmes for children. At the time of writing these include Children's BBC's Smart, Raven, Newsround, Bamzooki and Jackanory. What's even more encouraging is the latest evolution in computer game technology – the Nintendo Wii™. Using this games console involves players interacting with the screen using a hand-held device similar to a remote control. Playing games requires players to get up and move. In a game of tennis the Wii remote is your racquet and you swing the arm that's holding the device to make shots. In a driving game the remote acts as a steering wheel, which you have to move. Finally, in Big Brain Academy for Wii players are challenged to 'think, memorize, analyze, compute and identify' while on the move. On a number of levels this suits aspects of boys' learning styles. There is more about this in Section II.

Here are some ways to make watching television less passive when using it in the classroom:

- watch it standing up;
- allow movement while watching;
- stop the programme every five minutes and ask the children to discuss in pairs what's happened;
- stop the programme every ten minutes and give the children a count of 10 to change to a different seat;
- ask a question at the beginning of the programme that the children have to answer by the end;
- stop the programme every five minutes and ask pupils to make notes on what they consider the key points are;
- challenge the children to come up with one question, comment and idea by the end of the programme;
- ask the children to keep a tally of every time a key word is spoken or a key image appears;
- challenge the children to recount the key points of a programme in words, pictures or actions.

Magazines

A high-street newsagent is likely to stock in excess of a thousand different magazines and comics. A quick look on the shelves of a local store revealed the following:

- Comics for toddlers, for example *Noddy*: 23
- Comics for boys, for example *Beano*, *Action Man*: 39
- Comics for girls, for example *Sparkle*, *Mizz*, *Girl Talk*: 49.

Magazines for teenage girls were well represented with titles such as *Seventeen* and *Teen Vogue*. Teenage boys had nothing for them, apart from puzzle books.

In the men's special interest section I found thirty-eight leisure titles covering wrestling, climbing, combat, surfing and boxing; nineteen dedicated to football; eighteen about fishing; and thirteen about guns. In the section for women there were well over a hundred magazines dedicated to hair, cooking, crafts, getting married and being pregnant.

Finally, I found the following in the lifestyle section:

- Men's fashion and interest, for example *Gay Times*, *Esquire*, *Men's Fitness*, *FHM*: 26
- Women's fashion and interest, for example *Eve*, *Bella*, *Good Housekeeping*, *Psychologies*: 100

The quantity and quality of the magazines and comics a boy is exposed to will have an influence on the ideas he forms of what it is to be male, and how to relate to girls and women. What might he be thinking when he sees Kate Moss on the cover of *Vogue* or a rippling six-pack on the front of *Men's Health*? What conclusions might he draw about learning and behaviour from Dennis the Menace, Roger the Dodger and the Bash Street Kids when he opens a copy of the *Beano*? Will he be able to mitigate his experience of Sid the Sexist and Finbar Saunders in adult comics such as *Viz* as he gets older?

Boys and films

In the TV show presented by Richard Hammond mentioned earlier, one boy commented, 'Why bother reading *Lord of the Rings* when you can go and watch it at the cinema? It's quicker.' Others suggested it was hard work to create the images in your head from a book. A film version did the hard work for them.

Boys are visual learners and will be drawn to films.

Boys are visual learners and will be drawn to films. They will encounter a host of influential male characters in films, some of whom will feature in stories about school life. By the way these characters behave, boys may draw conclusions about how all boys behave in the classroom. The three lead characters in the Harry Potter films present clear learning stereotypes. Ron and Harry struggle to finish their homework – often leaving it to the last minute – have difficulty concentrating in lessons, moan about the quantity of homework / pending exams, and are in awe of Hermione's learning skills. Hermione, on the other hand, attends extra lessons and takes additional subjects, loves learning, hands homework in on time, engages with and remembers her learning, relishes exams, and despairs of Ron's and Harry's attitude to learning.

Ron and Harry do have excellent qualities that are depicted. It is important to make sure that the boys who watch these films or others that show boys in a school context do not overlook these merits.

Football

Football plays a big part in British culture and many boys think about little else. Their heroes play in the Premier League, and boys dream of representing their chosen club in the same way. These dreams are acted out daily on playgrounds as crowds of boys (and girls) chase balls enthusiastically.

It would be wise to use such dedication to a sport as a catalyst for learning. There are many programmes that do this with promising results. Libraries, schools, local authorities, football clubs and government organisations often collaborate on programmes aimed at getting boys reading. This may consist of a financial donation to buy books, a reading challenge based on the football league system or trained professionals setting up regular reading/football events.

Arsenal football club's Double Club gives boys from local schools access to teaching about basic literacy and numeracy skills through football. A clear and valued reward system is in place whereby fifty minutes of hard work and good classroom behaviour is recognised with a football coaching session. Chris Thomas, the Double Club teacher, believes that the motivation of such a prized reward is key to the club's success. He acknowledges that while some boys have no interest in working towards an achievement certificate, all of them are keen to get a coaching session or free match tickets and memorabilia.

It's important to remember that not every boy likes football and that there are other equally valuable sports that provide a bridge to learning too. As educators we need to identify and harness the enthusiasm that boys have for these activities and apply it to their learning.

Find out more:
http://www.arsenal.com
– select 'The Club'
followed by 'Community'

Boys, books and stories

Malorie Blackman, an author of fiction for children and teenagers, has said that she believes that boys find their way into a story's plot through the action, whereas girls enter via the characters. She recalled being told by a publisher that boys won't pick up a book if there's a girl on the cover, while girls aren't bothered whether there's a boy or girl. Garth Nix, another writer for children and teenagers, believes that boy readers need something extra to help them into a book. In his case, his publisher provided a CD on the cover of his novel *Mister Monday*.

Once boys become involved in reading, they encounter some interesting cultural influences on the male characters. Boys may well draw conclusions from these characters and their behaviour about what boys are like.

The table that follows shows the male and female characters that commonly appear in myths and fairy tales. These are usually among the first fictional characters that young children meet.

Male	Prince	Father	Warrior/Hunter	Wizard	King
Female	Princess	Mother	Adventurer	Witch	Queen

The traditional versions of these tales often present some interesting messages about gender. We meet the following characters in *Snow White and the Seven Dwarves*:

Snow White
female   does the housework
beautiful   looks after the males

Dwarves
male   perform hard manual labour
emotionally varied

Queen
female   evil and cunning
jealous of Snow White's beauty

Prince
handsome   brave
rescues Snow White

The same exercise is interesting when applied to *Little Red Riding Hood*:

Little Red Riding Hood
female   shrewd
brave   committed to caring for others

Grandma
female
helpless

Wolf
male   deceptive
evil

Woodcutter
male   strong
brave   protecting

The film *Hoodwinked* provides a fascinating retelling of the story of Red Riding Hood, with each main character telling the story from their own perspective. More importantly, these characters have been cleverly redrawn for the twenty-first century. Each one embodies a range of behaviours and attitudes from across the gender spectrum – for example, Grandma secretly indulges in competitive extreme sports.

The Dangerous Book for Boys by C. and H. Iggulden, which has proved very popular, gathers together a host of facts, advice and information deemed essential for any boy. It includes sections on conkers, catapults, spiders, building a tree-house, skimming stones, common British trees and the laws of cricket. This book is drawing on what boys were seen to be like sixty years ago. However, it also points the way to what they could be today. Interestingly, a similar book by Rosemary Davidson and Sarah Vine, *The Great Big Glorious Book for Girls*, is available for girls.

See also D. Enright's and G. MacDonald's *The Boys' Book: How to Be the Best at Everything* and its equivalent, Juliana Foster's *The Girls' Book: How to Be the Best at Everything*. Details of all these are on page 60.

"This will be a go-faster kart."

Section II:
I Want to Teach Boys Well

In Section I we created a clear and thorough picture of what makes a boy a boy. Now we'll use our creative professionalism to apply this knowledge in the classroom.

In Section II you'll have the opportunity to:
- revisit and summarise what you've learned about boys
- find out how to value their strengths
- plan for their unique challenges
- find out how to match their needs to specific types of classroom activity
- develop yourself as a teacher of boys
- create boy-friendly lessons and classrooms.

Chapter 6
I want to understand boys revisited

The following statements are not intended as excuses but reasons for boys' learning behaviour. Bear them in mind when you think about the boys you work with and how you can teach them well.

Brain wiring: Boys' brains grow differently from girls'. Boys have different learning preferences to girls. Boys are more prone to learning disorders such as dyslexia and autism.
Values: Boys will value different things from their educators. With guidance, boys' values will change over time. Boys' values drive their words and actions.
Family: Family expectations shape boys' self-belief. Family change/turbulence puts pressure on boys. Fathers / male carers influence boys' academic achievement.
School: Boys consistently underperform in comparison to girls. Assessment methods do not favour boys. Boys' experiences of school will tell them if they are successful or not.
Society: Boys get into more trouble and commit more crime than girls. Boys seek male guidance and initiation tasks in society. Boys contribute to society in many positive ways.
Culture: Boys are exposed to powerful role models on a daily basis. Television and computer games may influence boys' engagement with learning. Football and other sports may be a catalyst for raising boys' achievement.

The table describes typical boy behaviour, but every learner is unique. We must remember that a learning profile is as distinctive as a face.

Profiling

Personalised learning requires teachers to respond to the individual learning needs of pupils. We need effective ways to manage this. Profiling is a good way to start.

The quality of any personalised learning is dependent on the quality of the relationships between teacher and pupils. The strength of these associations determines how well a teacher knows their learners and therefore how well they can meet their needs. Profiling provides quick and practical ways for a teacher to learn about their learners. The six areas shown in the table above will help you do this. Building up a profile of each boy you work with in terms of these will help to inform your thinking and expectations. As a result, you will expect boys to behave differently from girls and be aware of the influences that may shape their interactions with you.

Next, we'll look at two different but complementary methods of profiling boys and their learning.
1. What their brains programme them to need while learning – learning styles.
2. What their brains programme them to do while learning – multiple intelligences.

Chapter 7
I want to value and use boys' strengths

When women are depressed they either eat or go shopping. Men invade another country.

Elayne Boosler, comedienne

Boys' learning needs (learning styles)

A boy's unique brain wiring will give him specific learning needs. It's easy to build these into lessons without disadvantaging the girls in your group. The following diagrams show facts to do with the brain wiring of boys on the left and consequences for the classroom on the right. The guidance should provide quick and effective means to engage with boys' learning preferences.

Boys have weaker neural connections in their temporal lobes than girls, which means they are less skilled at listening, especially to the tone of voice.	Pair girls with boys during listening tasks, and break frequently to ask pairs to tell each other in turn what's just been said. Challenge the girls to teach the boys how to listen well.
Because the hippocampus works differently in boys' brains, they need more time to memorise things. The hippocampus favours list-making – titles, headings, subheadings – and so detailed lists help boys to remember key points.	Challenge boys to distil a lesson into a set number of bulleted points. Build in time for boys to tell each other what they've learned. Ask children to write a list of what happened in the last lesson at the beginning of a new lesson.
Girls' frontal lobes are more active than boys'. Frontal lobes help a person to self-regulate. This means that boys are more likely than girls to make impulsive, risky decisions.	Create pressure with choices involving a time limit. Provide boys with opportunities to take risks and make quick decisions. For example, give them 20 seconds to draw or write a summary of a key point.
Two key language areas of the brain – Broca's and Wernicke's – develop later in boys. The male brain therefore uses fewer neural pathways for word production and expressing experience and emotion.	Explore this area using emotional recipes. Give boys three lists – one of emotions, one of vocabulary used for measuring, and one of actions that would be found in a recipe. Ask them to create a recipe for the best football match ever.
Girls have more oestrogen and oxytocin than boys. These hormones have a direct impact on the use of words. Boys have more testosterone, which drives aggression, and more vasopressin, which is linked to a male's concern about territoriality and hierarchy.	Allow boys to work and learn in competitive teams in which they establish different roles and responsibilities and have a home base to return to. Encourage them to discuss how they have organised their teams and give reasons for their decisions.
Boys have a larger and more active amygdala – a part of the brain's limbic system that registers emotional stimuli – than girls. They will react more quickly and aggressively to perceived or real threats.	Provide clear rules, safe cool-off areas and relaxation routines for boys. Teach them how to recognise and manage their anger and aggression through meditation, breathing routines and visualisation. **Visit www.heartmath.com**

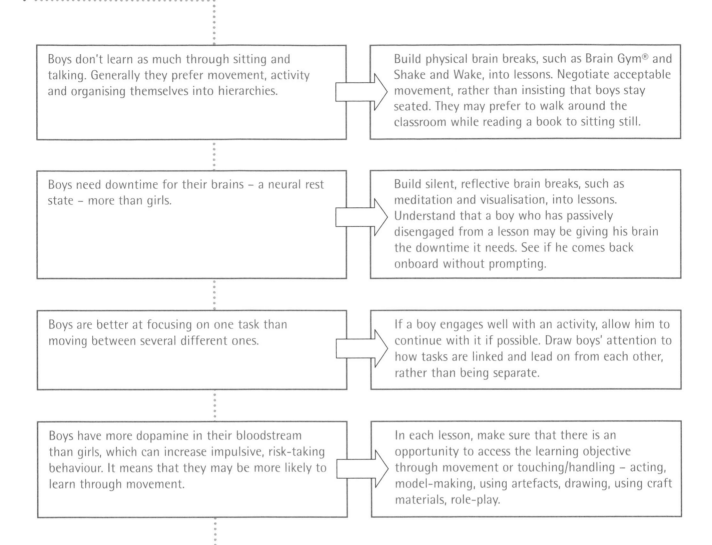

Boys don't learn as much through sitting and talking. Generally they prefer movement, activity and organising themselves into hierarchies.

Build physical brain breaks, such as Brain Gym® and Shake and Wake, into lessons. Negotiate acceptable movement, rather than insisting that boys stay seated. They may prefer to walk around the classroom while reading a book to sitting still.

Boys need downtime for their brains – a neural rest state – more than girls.

Build silent, reflective brain breaks, such as meditation and visualisation, into lessons. Understand that a boy who has passively disengaged from a lesson may be giving his brain the downtime it needs. See if he comes back onboard without prompting.

Boys are better at focusing on one task than moving between several different ones.

If a boy engages well with an activity, allow him to continue with it if possible. Draw boys' attention to how tasks are linked and lead on from each other, rather than being separate.

Boys have more dopamine in their bloodstream than girls, which can increase impulsive, risk-taking behaviour. It means that they may be more likely to learn through movement.

In each lesson, make sure that there is an opportunity to access the learning objective through movement or touching/handling – acting, model-making, using artefacts, drawing, using craft materials, role-play.

Building a group profile

Brain wiring (nature) is the driving force behind learning preferences, although environment (nurture) plays its part. As stated previously, individual learning-style preferences may be described using some form of learner profile. One of the most thorough of these is Barbara Prashnig's Learning Style Analysis, which addresses the new and difficult aspects of learning. By answering an online questionnaire, learners can discover their preferences in over twenty different areas. These are arranged into six categories:

- ◗ brain dominance – analytical versus holistic thinking
- ◗ sensory - visual, kinaesthetic, auditory, tactile
- ◗ physical – time of day, food intake, mobility
- ◗ environmental – temperature, light levels, background noise
- ◗ social – learning alone, with peer group, in a team
- ◗ attitudinal – motivation, persistence, conformity.

Find out more:
www.networkcontinuum.
co.uk/lsa

For further reading
Pocket PAL: Learning Styles and Personalized Teaching by Barbara Prashnig

What makes this system appealing is its group profile feature. The system allows the learning style profiles of a class or teaching group to be averaged to give a single profile. This profile describes the learning needs of a group, rather than of just one pupil. It's a quick and simple way to embark on developing personalised learning. For example, a group profile may tell us that the vast majority of learners in a class will learn new and/or difficult material more effectively if they can:

- ◯ discuss it with each other
- ◯ have access to reading material
- ◯ have access to visual support materials
- ◯ have the freedom to move about the work area
- ◯ work in teams under close supervision
- ◯ work in a warm classroom with the lights dimmed and no background noise.

The factors would therefore need to be taken into account when planning for such a group. The boys' learning needs are aggregated with the girls'. If a particular boy's needs fall outside the group profile, revisit his individual profile and adapt his learning accordingly.

Thousands of children have completed Prashnig's analysis, and some important gender differences have emerged, as the table that follows indicates.

Is it hot in here or is it us?

Primary-school findings

Boys	Girls
more impulsive	more reflective
greater need for movement	greater emphasis on auditory and visual learning
more likely to talk, less likely to listen	
more tactile	
prefer a cool environment	prefer a warm, formal environment

Informal research supports the idea that the majority of boys in a female teacher's classroom may feel too warm, and the majority of girls in a male teacher's classroom may feel too cold. Try asking your learners whether their working temperature is affecting their learning.

What boys do when they're learning (multiple intelligences)

A boy's unique skills and talents lead him to prefer some learning activities to others. Howard Gardner, professor of cognition and education at the Harvard Graduate School of Education, has developed a theory of multiple intelligences that provides a clear framework for identifying and using these abilities. Gardner argues there are at least eight distinct intelligences, each one based on a different set of human abilities. If you agree with his thinking, then it follows that everyone is intelligent and has a unique intelligences profile. Because we would be hard pressed to value one part of our brain more than another, each intelligence is given equivalent status. For example, musical ability, which is managed in part by areas of the right hemisphere, is as valuable as linguistic ability, which is managed generally by the left hemisphere.

The main different intelligences identified by Gardner are:

- ◓ Musical/Rhythmic – making and appreciating music
- ◓ Verbal/Linguistic – using language
- ◓ Existential – contemplating deep issues
- ◓ Naturalist – understanding and working with nature
- ◓ Interpersonal – managing relationships
- ◓ Intrapersonal – understanding oneself
- ◓ Visual/Spatial – perceiving and using images
- ◓ Mathematical/Logical – thinking and acting analytically
- ◓ Bodily/Kinaesthetic – using one's body.

Dr Branton Shearer, a world leader in the assessment and application of multiple intelligences, has studied the differences between boys' and girls' intelligences profiles. In one study he looked at 135 high-school students and discovered the following overall strengths:

Boys	Girls
Bodily/Kinaesthetic	Musical/Rhythmic
Mathematical/Logical	Verbal/Linguistic
Visual/Spatial	
Intrapersonal	Interpersonal
Naturalist	Naturalist

It is important not to assume that all boys are only bodily/kinaesthetic, mathematical/logical, visual/spatial, interpersonal and naturalist learners. These different intelligences represent tendencies only; each boy will have his own unique mix of all the intelligences. However, while more research is needed in this area, Dr Shearer's findings relate well to our intuitive and day-to-day knowledge of how boys are. With this in mind, here are some activities to build into lessons that will support the preferred intelligences of boys.

Intelligence	What a boy will want to do
Bodily/Kinaesthetic	Move, touch, handle, build, make, construct
Mathematical/Logical	Think, ask questions, seek order, have reasons, know the learning objective and lesson format
Visual/Spatial	Watch, imagine, create, visualise, paint, draw, watch television, look at photographs, read graphic novels
Intrapersonal	Be independent, work alone, have their own space, set and monitor their own targets
Naturalist	Explore, classify, identify patterns in nature, relate to surroundings

If you feel that the boys you are working with are not co-operating, the following table may help you to consider whether their misbehaviour is an unrecognised or underused intelligence seeking expression and appreciation.

Intelligence	Possible misbehaviour
Musical/Rhythmic	Humming, rhythmic tapping
Verbal/Linguistic	Talking at inappropriate times, a desire to have the last word, general cheekiness
Existential	Asking challenging and provocative questions, general rebellion
Naturalist	Leaving the classroom to go outside without permission
Interpersonal	Valuing friends more than lessons, refusing to work independently
Intrapersonal	Refusing to work with others, moody, not engaging with lesson
Visual/Spatial	Daydreaming
Mathematical/Logical	Arguing, a desire to have the last word
Bodily/Kinaesthetic	Squirming on seat, getting up from seat without permission, fiddling with something

Find out more:
www.thinkingclassroom.co.uk

For further reading
Pocket PAL: Multiple Intelligences by Mike Fleetham

Like Learning Styles Analysis, multiple intelligences can be assessed online using the MIDAS assessment and a group profile can be generated for a class or teaching group.

What boys tell us about learning

Boys might be able to tell you how they learn best, but if they can't yet, then their preferences will be revealed through their learning behaviour. If they respond well to an activity, that activity is probably aligned to their learning strengths. If they disengage and switch off, they're asking for something different. Without realising it, through their preferences boys are telling us a great deal about good teaching and learning.

Research conducted by the National Training Laboratory in the United States indicates the impact that different types of learning have on the retention of information. As the following table indicates, the more effective methods of learning involve getting up and doing something, rather than sitting and listening or watching. Interestingly, that's exactly what many boys are telling us they need – to be actively involved in their learning.

Lynne: It was worth pairing boys with girls even though I had to battle with verbal complaints from boys and seething, silent looks from girls. Using multiple intelligences and learning styles helped. Talking about how we can complement each other as learners made it more neutral and acceptable.

Jo: I felt it had become unfashionable to say that boys and girls were different and now, thankfully, it feels like we can say it again. I sometimes find myself apologising for my twins' boyish behaviour. However, when this behaviour is channelled properly and in appropriate settings, I am proud of their energy and enthusiasm for life.

Arthur: I don't get into trouble at school much. Other boys get into trouble for not listening and for talking and for being annoying.

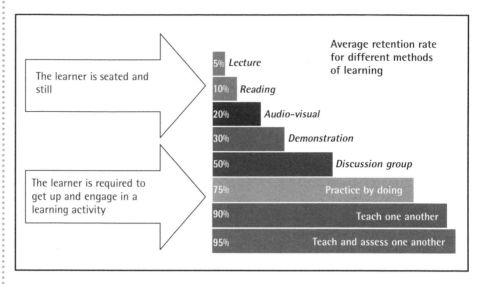

National Training Laboraties, Bethel, Maine, USA

Chapter 8
I want to support boys in their challenges

We've looked at boys' learning strengths using learning styles and multiple intelligences profiles. We'll now turn our attention to the common challenges that boys face in their lives and learning, and how we can help.

Emotional intelligence and self-confidence

Panorama once produced the programme *The Future is Female*. During it, a 7-year-old boy was asked 'What would you say about a boy who works well in school?' He answered, 'He's not a boy.' The programme went on to draw the conclusion that if boys see girls working hard, then working hard makes them a girl. In the magazine *Junior Education*, Audrey McIlvain discovered similar attitudes during a small-scale study into the thoughts of Year-6 boys. Amongst other things, the boys told her 'It's not cool to work hard' and 'it's not cool to show you are worried and upset.'

Boys may lack the brain machinery to recognise and express their emotions as effectively as girls. In addition, their confidence and self-esteem may suffer when they feel they are living in the academic shadow of girls. Here are some ways to improve boys' emotional intelligence and self-esteem.

Give appropriate praise
Research from the Tavistock Institute of Human Relations indicates that it takes at least four positive comments to counter the emotional damage caused by one negative comment. The research also highlights that the ratio of negative to positive comments in a typical classroom can be as high as 5 to 1. That means there's a lot of praise needed!

There are five straightforward rules for giving praise, which are these:
1. Decide whether private or public praise is most appropriate and give it accordingly. Some boys will not thank you for making a public show of praising them. A quiet word at the end of the lesson may be much more constructive.
2. Give specific praise that makes clear what has been done well —'Excellent learning. You've really got the hang of "-ight" words. Well done.'
3. Instead of praise being a destination, it should point to the next stage of the learning journey — 'Excellent learning. You've really got the hang of "-ight" words. I think you'll have no problem with "-ough" ones now.'
4. Praise the learning, not the learner: Praising the learner diverts attention away from the learning taking place. Even when progress is more personal, still address the learning — 'Well done, you've got far more control over your anger. Good effort.'

5. Turn errors into targets by focusing on the positives. There's nothing wrong with making a mistake or giving an incorrect answer. In fact, errors give far more information about how you can help than successes do. Try the following:
    - 'You're partly right, now think a bit more.'
    - 'Not quite, so have another go.'
    - 'I see why you gave that answer. I'm looking for something different. I want you to have another go.'
    - 'Nearly, but have you considered …'

Notice that the learner will know that they haven't got it right, but that the emphasis is on moving to the correct answer rather than dwelling on the error.

Strategic praise can be very effective. Subtle, well-planned and targeted private praise is a shrewd way to reach those whom others consider to be the ring leaders in your class. If the dominant male in the class promotes a culture of non-achievement that the other males are following, then excite him about learning through short, direct and private praise. Maybe, just maybe, he'll begin to value learning, prompting the other boys to adopt an 'It's cool to be clever' classroom culture.

"There is always something to value and celebrate, however well hidden it may be."

Value them for what they do well

Try to focus on what each boy does well and let him know verbally or through an established praise and reward system that you are aware of it. If you're struggling to find the positives for a particular boy – an experience we've all had – use different starting points to find something that's praiseworthy. Try considering each aspect of their learning style, each of the multiple intelligences or each curriculum area. There is always something to value and celebrate, however well hidden it may be.

Make clear how to succeed and make success achievable

Boys' logical nature requires us to provide them with clear criteria for success. Boys will respond best when such criteria are broken down into small and manageable steps. If you involve boys in negotiating what these success criteria will be, the response will be even better. For example, if you want boys to have better quality playtimes, ask them 'What would a passer-by see and hear us doing if we were having a perfect playtime?' Make a list of all their suggestions, which might include:

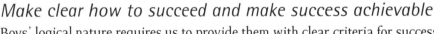

- everyone in the correct part of the playground
- no dropping of litter
- older children helping younger ones
- playground games taking place
- excited but not aggressive behaviour
- only one game of football taking place.

> **Lynne:** I had boys in my class who were quietly desperate to please and to be liked and valued by me, but they knew this wasn't considered 'cool' and wanted to keep their 'top dog' status. One untimely piece of public praise from me could have ruined the rapport that was developing between us.

> **Jo:** My sons like to come home with evidence that they have behaved well or have learned something new. At their school this comes in the form of green slips and stickers. They are something to show for their efforts, and something to act as a bit of healthy competition.

> **Arthur:** My teacher told me that what I did was really good. She said she was proud of me for my picture fairy-tale book. The first picture I did was so good that she said I could show it to the art teacher. She teaches Year 5 and she said that some of her class couldn't draw a castle like that.

Thanks to Chris Dickinson for this activity.

Next, ask the boys to choose the five most important points from the list. Tell them that you will be monitoring the playground to see if any of the chosen criteria are being met. Explain that you are hoping to reward those children who are following the chosen points.

Such involvement in decision-making gives boys the opportunity to talk, discuss, debate, use higher-order thinking, evaluate and collaborate.

Tell the boys that you admire and value them

Take calculated risks in the way you praise and value the boys you work with. Dare to use words like 'admire' and 'proud'. If this feels a little uncomfortable for you, pick your moment and recipient carefully, note the impact of your words and then decide whether it's worth adopting as a strategy. Here are some scripts for you to practise before using them in school.

- ◯ 'I admire the way you stuck at that problem and saw it through.'
- ◯ 'I'm proud of you because you got your temper under control.'
- ◯ 'I admire you for making such an effort with your reading as I know you find it difficult.'
- ◯ 'I'm really proud of you for improving your attendance at school.'

Try to overcome any feelings of awkwardness as there's a strong likelihood that you will be the first person to say something like this to some of the boys you teach.

Help boys to develop the language of emotions

In its simplest form, emotional intelligence is about three things:
1. recognising your emotions
2. naming your emotions
3. expressing your emotions appropriately.

Owing to their brain wiring, boys will need help in all three areas.

Emotional recipes

We can begin by drawing on some of the strengths of boys – their ability to order, structure and categorise.
1. Ask the boys to list all the words and phrases they know that express quantity, both standard and non-standard measures. Give them two minutes only to do this. Bring in some recipe books for reference.
2. Next, ask them to list words and phrases that describe what someone does when cooking – for example, whisk, stir. Again, limit this to two minutes.
3. Finally, using a list of emotions, such as in the table that follows, challenge the boys to prepare a recipe for the best football match ever. Tell them they have ten minutes to do this, before they share what they have prepared with the class.

Make sure that you differentiate this activity as required, giving support where it is needed. A couple of examples of the style required follow. You can use them for guidance if you need to:

○ 'Take a pinch of expectation and mix it with a pint of enthusiasm' – getting ready to leave for the match.

○ 'Slice off 100 g of despair and fry it quickly in a tablespoon of rage' – one of your team's players misses a penalty.

List of emotions

admiration	desire	exhilaration	hysteria	relief
adoration	despair	expectation	impatience	remorse
amazement	desperation	fascination	indifference	resentment
ambition	determination	fear	indignation	respect
anger	disappointment	frustration	infatuation	revenge
anticipation	disbelief	greed	jealousy	sadness
anxiety	disgust	grief	joy	shame
awe	disillusionment	guilt	loneliness	shock
bewilderment	eagerness	happiness	mischief	sorrow
boredom	embarrassment	hatred	panic	suspicion
compassion	enthusiasm	hope	pity	sympathy
contempt	envy	hopelessness	pride	terror
curiosity	exaltation	horror	rage	weariness
defiance	exasperation	humiliation	regret	worry

Model emotional literacy

One of the best ways to teach emotional literacy is to model it. This doesn't mean that you have to share your inner self. However, it does mean that you might occasionally talk about how you're feeling and why. If you do so, never speak in a way that implies that you feel the children you are addressing are responsible for your emotions – 'You're really making me angry' needs to be replaced with 'I'm feeling angry because this lesson is not going to plan.' Make sure that your comments cover a range of emotions, including positive ones. When you start sharing a little of your own life, you'll have the undivided attention of every single member of your class, boy or girl.

Provide safe areas

If you want boys to express their emotions appropriately, you need to prepare for how you will handle the emotions that are more difficult to manage, especially anger. It's important for boys to know that there is nothing wrong with feeling angry. However, what might need to change is the way they express it. Draw their attention to the outward signs of anger – clenched fists and jaw, sweating, raised heartbeat, shouting, faster breathing. Then provide them with safe alternatives to lashing out when they recognise their anger. These ways should allow them to keep their pride intact. Suggest the following strategies:

- Actions: walk away to a safe place, count to 10, find a trusted friend/teacher to talk to.
- Scripts: use sentences such as 'I feel really angry about what's happened. I'm going to walk away because I'm in control.'
- Ways of expressing anger in a safe and private area: punch a cushion, rip a newspaper to shreds, cry, shout, write, draw.

Use reflective language

When a boy is explaining how he is feeling, try to include some of his own words in your responses. This not only values their emotional literacy, but develops their communication skills as well. For example:

Child: I'm cross.
Teacher: Can you tell me why you're cross?
Child: I'm not happy because Damien took my football.
Teacher: So you're unhappy about what Damien did, are you? Tell me more.

Note that at each stage, the teacher includes the child's words in their response.

Use humour

Here are some telling jokes about how males act and perceive themselves. The first is by the comedian Dylan Moran, who is recounting a phone conversation; and the second is an interaction between a comedian, Bill Bailey, and his audience:

Son: Dad, I love you.
Father: You OK for money, son?
Son: No, Dad, I love you.
Father: Right. Good, I'll go and get your mother.

Are there any men in tonight?
Silence, a few giggles.
Are there any women in tonight?
Women call out loudly.
Are there any blokes in tonight?
Men now call out loudly.

Boys like humour and, with careful management and suitable ground rules, it can be a powerful ally to your teaching. Once you feel confident with a group, introduce an occasional joke now and again.

Boys will be in their element if you allow them to tell jokes. This is excellent for speaking and listening skills. You could set aside some time for this, calling it the Stand-up Club.

Another way to infuse humour into the classroom is to establish a joke board, with clear criteria for what types of jokes will be accepted for display. The following list worked well in my classrooms. The joke must be:

- legibly written
- spelled accurately
- grammatically accurate
- one that makes sense
- clean, not rude

- funny
- no longer than two hundred words
- illustrated
- no larger than A5
- approved by the humour inspector – me.

When a boy is explaining how he is feeling, try to include some of his own words in your responses.

You'll notice that the guidelines mean that any boys seeking to enter will have to meet some writing targets.

Laughter can be hugely beneficial. In my work in schools, I find consistently that the happiest teachers have the happiest children. Humour also has strong links with learning – the feeling you have when you 'get' a joke is similar to the one you have when you 'get' something new in terms of learning.

Raise your expectations of boys

This one's very easy to say, but hard to do. It is vital to helping boys in school. This whole book is dedicated to helping you see boys in a positive way and thereby raise your expectations of them. It is summed up in the following Native American saying:

If you aim your arrow at the moon, you may just hit an eagle.
If you aim your arrow at an eagle, it may just fall onto the rocks.

Help boys to develop their communication skills

Run learning circles

This is one of my favourite learning activities because it plays to many of the strengths of boys, yet develops their weaknesses at the same time. It involves a clear structure, purposeful movement, thinking skills, individual work, writing, speaking, listening, turn-taking and co-operation. A learning circle may be made up of six to ten children. It's fine to have an empty seat if the numbers don't work out exactly. Here's how a circle works when applied to a topic review. It has many other uses too.

❍ Give each participant a piece of A5 paper or a large Post-it® note.

❍ Allow two minutes' silent, individual writing time to answer a question you pose – such as 'What have you learned about … over the last … ?'

❍ Arrange the children in appropriate-sized groups and ask them to form a learning circle, bringing their notes with them. The diagram shows a circle for a group of 8.

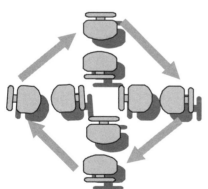

❍ Children sitting in the inner chairs of the circle are 'talkers' and those sitting in the outer circle are 'listeners'.

❍ Give the talkers thirty seconds to tell the listeners (outer) what they have learned, using their notes if they wish.

❍ After thirty seconds, ask those sitting in the outer circle to move round one chair in a clockwise direction so that they are facing a new talker.

❍ Talkers have a further thirty seconds to share their learning with their new partner. Repeat this until the listeners have heard all the talkers in their group.

❍ Now ask the talkers and listeners in each group to swap seats and repeat the activity with the roles reversed.

By the end of a learning circle every pupil will have rehearsed their learning many times and enhanced their speaking and listening skills. A circle takes no more than ten minutes. It's easy to assess children's understanding by moving between circles; as a new child comes within earshot, you can make brief notes about what they are saying. Thanks to Jack Drury for this activity.

Here are some of the other ways in which a learning circle may be used.

Inner circle roles	Outer circle
Characters from history – research biographical information beforehand	Historical investigators/inquisitors – prepare suitable questions beforehand
Different countries – research geographical facts beforehand	Explorers – prepare suitable questions beforehand
Teachers of different multiplication tables – prepare strategies earlier	Learners of multiplication facts
Teachers of spelling rules – prepare strategies in advance	Learners of spelling rules
Famous artists exhibiting their latest work – research information beforehand	Interviewers for an art magazine – prepare suitable questions beforehand

Lynne: We designed posters featuring two football players confronting each other. They depicted different emotions and enabled discussion using a familiar context for the boys. When both players were red in the face, it was suggested that they walk away. Jokes also featured and were incorporated into impromptu talent shows.

Jo: I agree that boys love to be competitive and sort out who is top dog in their class. Unusually, but fortunately, my sons are among a group of boys who have decided that it is cool to be on a higher-level reading book than other children. Competition can sometimes be a good thing.

Thanks to the Critical Skills Programme for this activity. www.criticalskills.co.uk

Arthur: We go and get stuff for lessons and when we do maths we stand up to do actions to our times tables. When we go to sit at our tables we can move around for a bit. We stand up to take our coats off.

Provide scripts

Lev Vygotsky, the Russian psychologist, gave the world of education many valuable things including scaffolding. This is not the tea-drinking-workmen-with-a-flat-bed-lorry-blocking-your-drive scaffolding, but educational scaffolding. Just as real scaffolding provides structure and support around an emerging building, educational scaffolding gives structure and support around a developing learner. And when the learner is strong enough, like a completed building, the scaffolding is removed.

If boys have trouble finding the right things to say, we should provide them with structure and support. A partial script will help with this. The one that follows will help a boy talk about a lesson. All he needs to do is to fill in the blanks and rehearse what he's going to say with another boy before telling a bigger group.

'I have been learning about … . It's important because … . My aim was to … . By the end of the lesson I hoped to … . I decided to use … to make a … . My final product was … . Overall my feelings about this lesson are … . What I valued most was … .'

You can adapt this basic scaffold to suit other circumstances.

Define good communication

Earlier, we saw how to involve boys in negotiating their own success criteria (see page 38). The same ideas can be applied to communication. Ask the boys you teach what a visitor to the classroom would see and hear if 'classy communication' were taking place. Develop a list with them and remember to add to the list key behaviours that they may not have identified.

"I think that's the new lining-up sign."

Use non-verbal communication

Boys are less disposed to listening than girls and more tuned into visual and kinaesthetic communication, so develop some alternative methods of classroom communication using some of the following options:

- sounds
- hand signals
- whole-body actions
- facial expressions
- images and symbols
- objects
- music.

The following table shows how each one of these might be used for common classroom instructions.

Instruction / Method	'Line up, please.'	'Listen, please.'	'Sit on the carpet, please.'	'Tidy up, please.'
Instrumental sound	Ring a bell.	A single drumbeat	Shake a shaker.	Play a triangle.
Hand signal	Perform a karate-chop action.	Cup ear with hand.	Slap thighs.	Wiggle fingers in front of you.
Whole-body action	Put arms in the air. Stand on tiptoe.	Do the twist.	Sit down on the carpet yourself.	Run on the spot.
Facial expression	Make an exaggerated smile.	Form a series of silent Os with your mouth.	Wrinkle nose.	Puff out cheeks.
Image and/ or symbol	Hold up a photo of a straight line of children.	Hold up a photo of a person listening well.	Hold up a picture of a carpet.	Hold up a picture of a skip.
Object	Hold up a ruler.	Hold up a fake plastic ear.	Hold up a carpet tile.	Hold up a dustpan and brush.
Music	'The Finish Line' by Snow Patrol	'Do You Want to Know a Secret' by the Beatles – starts with the word 'listen'	'Sittin' on the Dock of the Bay' by Otis Redding	Theme tune to *The Benny Hill Show*

It's best if you develop your own non-verbal cues with your class, taking their ideas on board. Non-verbal communication is an effective way to play to boys' strengths as well as enriching your relationship with all the learners in your group.

Develop collaborative groupwork/teamwork

Boys' brains are programmed to be aware of hierarchy, territoriality and competition. We can exploit these strengths by setting competitive learning challenges using collaborative teams with defined roles for members and clear reporting structures. Here's how it works:

- Split your class into groups of up to 6.
- Define the roles that are needed for each team to succeed.
- Allocate roles and responsibilities, and explain the reporting structure within each team.
- Define the ground rules.
- Issue a challenge.
- Set success criteria.
- The challenge commences.
- Judge the results.
- Celebrate the winning team.
- Value the efforts of all teams.
- Agree targets for improvement.

Here's an example of a competitive learning challenge in action.

- Split the children into groups of up to 6, depending on the class's age and maturity. If you allow the children to sort out the groups, point out that a range of skills will be needed for success, so friendship groups may not be the best choice.
- Define the roles that are needed for a team to succeed – leader (not boss), reporter, writer, materials manager, timer and checker.
- Allocate roles and responsibilities, and explain the reporting structure within each team.
  - *Leader*
    Makes sure everyone has a job to do.
    Makes sure everyone has their say.
    Makes sure everyone is feeling OK.
  - *Reporter*
    Communicates with teacher on behalf of their group.
    Speaks to whole class on behalf of their group.
  - *Writer*
    Takes notes when needed.
    Produces any written material required as part of the challenge.
  - *Materials manager*
    Keeps working area tidy.
    Obtains the tools and materials needed.
  - *Timer*
    Informs team of time elapsed and time remaining at regular intervals.
  - *Checker*
    Makes sure that team members are performing as expected.
    Makes sure that the challenge is being fulfilled.
- Define ground rules
  - Everyone in a group reports to their leader.
  - The leader is responsible for looking after their team members and attempting to meet the challenge.
- Issue a challenge
  - Take thirty minutes to create a presentation about forces in science using any materials readily available in the classroom, and produce ten bullet points that summarise what you know.
- Set success criteria
  - A presentation should last no more than two minutes.
  - The ten bullet points must be spelled correctly.
  - Everyone must take part in the presentation in some way.
- The challenge commences
  - Allow thirty minutes for preparation, during which you can assess teamwork, make notes and coach where needed.

○ Judge the results
  • Presentations are performed and assessed against the success criteria.
○ Celebrate the winning team
  • The winning team receives an appropriate reward.
○ Value the efforts of all teams
  • Each team should receive praise for what they did well.
○ Agree targets for improvement
  • Each team decides what they could improve upon for next time.

If you find that the boys in your group are not ready to work at this level, build up slowly with smaller challenges and smaller teams.

Boys need to find a role that they're good at in these challenges – natural leaders need to be in charge, effective writers need to be reporters, those who are naturally organised should be material managers. Once children have experienced success in one role, rotate the roles so that they have a chance to develop different skills.

When boys are comfortable in one team, rearrange the groups to change the dynamics. Geoff Hannan, an expert in boys' learning, recommends that learners spend a third of their groupwork/teamwork time in each of the following configurations:

○ mixed gender, non-friendship groups   ○ friendship groups.
○ single gender, non-friendship groups

Literacy
Reading
Here are four 'Dos' to help with boys' reading.

1. Assume that boys want to read fiction

Boys do want to read fiction, but it needs to be the right fiction.

Boys do want to read fiction, but it needs to be the right fiction. Garth Nix believes that writers should not try to create books especially for boys. Rather, they should concentrate on producing good fiction that engages readers. He says that once boys have had a helping hand into a book, then they'll be away. We need to help boys to identify books they will like. Try choosing a class reader that you think boys will enjoy. After hearing you read they may be inspired to seek out other work by the same author. Try books by Garth Nix, Anthony Horowitz, Philip Pullman, Joseph Delaney and Angie Sage.

2. Use boys' desire for order and hierarchy
These will help you to teach boys to read in an explicit and structured way. Tell them about how reading works and why you're teaching them a particular aspect, as opposed to simply doing it to them with no explanation. Teach them how phonics works, tell them how many different phonemes there are (44), explain that there are about 230 graphemes to represent these sounds. Boys like facts and numbers such as the following.

Language	Number of phonemes (spoken units of language)	Number of graphemes (written units of language)
English	44	Around 230
Italian	25	33

Explain the structure and hierarchy of written language and how it all fits together – graphemes, words, phrases, sentences, paragraphs, whole pieces.

3. Remember language disorders

Keep in mind boys' greater tendency to reading disorders such as dyslexia. Although boys will often acquire language skills later than girls, we must not fall into the trap of saying 'Oh, they're just boys. They'll catch up eventually' because maybe they won't. Contrary to popular belief, it's possible to identify the early signs of dyslexia in children as young as 5 years old. Such children need to be closely monitored to ensure than they make age-appropriate progress. If they don't, specialist intervention should take place immediately.

4. Model good reading

Boys need to see what an effective male reader looks like. They also need to see their reading role models successfully enjoying books and other reading material. Invite some of the following male readers into your classroom to work with boys who need a helping hand:

- ◗ older boys from the same school
- ◗ older boys from a different school (primary or secondary)
- ◗ male teachers
- ◗ male support staff – teaching assistants, site manager, midday meal staff
- ◗ dads and male carers
- ◗ granddads
- ◗ male relatives
- ◗ local businessmen
- ◗ university students.

Make sure that you check your school's policy and procedures for welcoming and vetting school visitors before issuing any invitations.

A structured hour-long session within the normal classroom routine or as a separate session might run as follows:

- ◗ The visiting readers share what they have been reading since the last session.
- ◗ The boys share what they have been reading since the last session.
- ◗ The visitors and boys pair up and read together, discussing their previous reading target.

Lynne: Tasks which involve teamwork, especially if they have a significant practical element, give the opportunity for boys who had previously felt failure to show skills of leadership, management and organisation. A sense of competition – even if only against the clock – really motivated them. I used digital photography to capture these times.

Jo: Competition certainly motivates my sons. As long as it does not become personal rivalry, I feel it's good training for life.

Arthur: There are seven men teachers in my school. Two are supply teachers. I saw Mr Jones reading a book in assembly once. There are thousands of ladies in school.

"Do you think there will be biscuits today?"

○ Include a brain break or reward – a short game of football for the boys / a snack / a short television show / some ICT time.

○ Both groups set a reading target for the next session.

A member of staff should monitor the session. The visitors could be offered basic guidelines for reading support. Do what you can with the time and resources available to you.

Writing

When it comes to writing, there are many ways to overcome boys' natural resistance. Here are a couple to get you started.

1. Writing frames

A writing frame provides the linguistic scaffolding that boys need. For example, if we want to teach a boy how to devise a valid argument, we could provide him with a writing frame. The second writing frame is for use with young boys who need help in writing a short report.

I want to argue in favour of _____

I have a number of reasons for my position.

My first reason is _____

My second reason is_____

Finally,_____

Therefore, although I appreciate that others may disagree, I think that

_____

We went to _____

On the way I saw_____

I enjoyed _____

I didn't enjoy_____

I learned about _____

Next time I'd like to visit _____

---

2. *2, 3, 5, 1*

In 2, 3, 5, 1 children think carefully in pairs about a small number of words that they are required to write. It necessitates thinking, talking, collaborating, evaluating and writing, but in such a way that boys won't be put off. This is how it works:

○ Arrange children in pairs.

○ Give some form of stimulus / source material.

○ Ask the pairs to explore the source material in any way (or ways) that is appropriate.

○ Challenge the pairs to summarise the source material in the following ways: one sentence, five words, and, finally, one word.

○ Set a strict yet appropriate time limit.

The source material may be anything that's linked to an appropriate learning objective for your group, such as a set of photos, a series of numbers, an artefact or a poem.

In case you are wondering: 2 stands for pairs, 3 for the different responses, 5 for the first summary, and 1 for a sentence/word.

Single-gender teaching

This is controversial and perhaps not an option in your school, but the research on the effectiveness of single-gender teaching is compelling. Michael Gurian cites several major international studies, including one from Australia that followed over 250,000 students for six years. Children in single-gender classrooms scored between 15 and 22 per cent higher in test scores than those working in mixed-sex environments. Studies in English public schools and American state schools have found similar gains. Researchers at Homerton College, Cambridge, are also investigating this topic. They have embarked on a three-year project to discover if the same is true of English state schools. I have a pretty good idea of what they'll find.

Behaviour

Boys need to know the rules. They want to know where they stand and exactly what will happen if they transgress. Moreover, if they do, they need certainty of follow-up, which is far more important than the severity of it.

In McIlvain's study, a group of boys said that they liked systems for behaviour. If you haven't got classroom and school behaviour systems already in place, this is worth exploring.

In addition to formal behaviour systems, each classroom will have its own working practices – interpretations and adaptations of the rules. An experienced teacher will be skilled at managing the evolution of such rules.

Good classroom management goes a long way towards reducing the need for behaviour management. If boys are engaged in purposeful learning activities that are matched to their strengths, they will be far less likely to be disruptive. However, the following guidance will be helpful for when they do need managing.

Give clear instructions

Boys don't listen as well as girls and are eager to be on the move, so it's important to give them clear, direct and unambiguous instructions. These directions need to be brief and to the point. It may help to monitor how many things you ask boys to do at one time. If you say the following: 'Finish your work, put your pencils away, tidy your desk and come and sit down, thanks', you are expecting your pupils to remember quite a lot, especially if one of them is a boy with dyslexia.

Find out more: www.standards.dfes.gov.uk/genderandachievement/understanding/singlesex/

Lynne: Academic results may have been higher in the single-gender studies, but what about attitudes towards and social interactions with the opposite sex? Will it perpetuate chauvinistic attitudes? How could this be prevented?

Jo: As long as there is plenty of interaction between boys and girls in school, there's a lot to be said for tailoring teaching to their particular style.

Arthur: I would say teaching boys and girls with different teachers is good because the teachers will have less children to look after. They should be separated into different classes and be taught their weakest skills. The strongest teachers should go with the naughtiest children.

You could achieve the same result using non-verbal communication, as mentioned on page 44, or by simplifying what you say, such as 'Tidy up, then on the carpet, thanks. That's two things, OK?'

Boys are keen to be given reasons for an instruction, so try to include them when appropriate –'Come and sit down, thanks. We need to plan for tomorrow.'

Boys are keen to be given reasons for an instruction.

Plan for levels of escalation

It may be tempting to respond to boys' misbehaviour by fighting back, giving as good as you get. To avoid this, take things step by step. You may find it helpful to move through the following stages at a speed that suits the situation:

- strategic ignoring
- simple direction
- simple choices
- consequential choices
- time out
- removal from class.

Here is an example of how this may work in practice with a child (Aaron) who is causing low-level but persistent disruption by tapping his pencil on the desk when he doesn't need the pencil.

Strategic ignoring
• Wait one minute to see if he stops.

If he doesn't …

Simple direction
• 'Aaron, pencil on the table, thanks.'

If he doesn't comply …

Simple choices
• 'Aaron, pencil on the table or in your tray, thanks.'

If he continues to tap his pencil …

Consequential choices
• 'Aaron, pencil away or you'll have time out.'

If he fails to stop …

Time out
'Aaron, you've chosen to ignore my instruction. Five minutes time out, thanks.'

If he fails to go to the time-out area of the classroom …

Removal from class
Aaron is escorted from the class. Reclaim the lesson calmly.

If you need to remove a child from the classroom, make sure you know your school's or LA's policy on such matters.

It may help to know what you are going to say if and when boys require firm handling.

Rehearse scripts

It may help to know what you are going to say if and when boys require firm handling. If you've rehearsed what you're going to say, there's less chance of your saying something you might later regret. It's also more likely that you will remain in control of both the situation and your own emotions if you do this. Here are some tips to bear in mind as you prepare scripts for the situations that are relevant for you:

❍ Use first names.

❍ Allow a pause after using a name to gain attention.

❍ Make brief eye contact.

❍ Give the direction succinctly.

❍ Say 'thanks' to indicate that you are assuming compliance, rather than 'please', which suggests you are anticipating it.

❍ Reclaim the lesson.

Here's an example of how these tips work in practice:
'Aaron, [pause, make eye contact] gum in the bin, thanks.' Look away and continue the lesson.

If this doesn't have the desired effect, you will need to refer to your plans for escalation (see page 50).

Practise this at home with your children or partner, or in the mirror.

Defuse with humour

If the misdemeanours are pretty insignificant, yet still need to be recognised by you – which is important for boys – try reframing the situation by using humour. I remember a turning point with a tricky Year-5 class when I started to use a catchphrase from a character in *The Simpsons*. I used it only occasionally and to address a specific behaviour so that it kept its shelf life and effectiveness, and it didn't look as if I was trying to be cool by overusing it.

The hit comedy show *Little Britain* is rated 15 for mild language and comic sex references and is watched by many 8–15-year-olds. Whatever your views on this programme, it offers a wealth of catch-phrases that can be used in the classroom with careful thought. Try the following:

❍ 'Computer says "No".'

❍ 'I don't like it.'

❍ 'Margaret!'

There are many other catch-phrases which find their way into common usage that you can adapt if you're not happy to use these ones. You need only listen in the playground to get a few ideas.

Protect pride

Whatever rules a boy has broken, it's essential that you do not damage his pride or dent his ego. He needs to know that you are unhappy with what he has done but that you still accept him. You should separate the boy from his behaviour. Therefore 'You are a disrespectful boy' is inappropriate, while 'Your attitude and words are disrespectful' is fine.

It is easy to get trapped in a no-win situation which will end up damaging a boy's pride and harming your relationship with him. The following conversation is an example of this.

> 'Stop chewing that gum right now.'
> 'No, I'm hungry.'
> 'You've got five seconds to put it in the bin or you'll miss fifteen minutes of Golden Time.'
> 'So, don't even like Golden Time.'
> 'You lose fifteen minutes.'
> 'I'm out of here.'

We have all probably been in this situation, and it could be handled differently with some forethought. Here's an alternative:

> 'I'm going to wander back over here in one minute. By then I expect the gum to be in the bin.'

Deliver this as a passing comment directed quietly to the child in question. By managing this situation in this way, the boy can put his gum in the bin unobserved by you and return to his seat. When you return exactly a minute later, a wink, nod or quiet word of thanks should resolve a potentially volatile situation.

Motivation and concentration

There's an urban myth that learners can only concentrate on something for a set number of minutes, this being their age plus or minus 2. So, in theory, an 8-year-old boy can concentrate on adjectives for between six and ten minutes. Allegedly, this measure peaks at the age of 20. A more realistic view assumes that learners will concentrate in proportion to their interest and motivation. In light of this, some schools teach boys in short bursts. Compare the following standard lesson with the framework that proceeds it:

◗ presentation of learning objective

◗ introduction

◗ 40-minute activity

◗ plenary.

Instead of this, some schools have opted for a framework broken into smaller parts, like this:

- presentation of overall learning objective
- short task
- introduction
- bite-sized learning objective
- 10-minute activity
- review
- brain break – Brain Gym or another physical activity or game
- bite-size learning objective

- 10-minute activity
- review
- bite-size learning objective
- 10-minute activity
- brain break – Brain Gym or another physical activity or game
- review
- plenary.

The ideas that we've explored in this chapter aim to 'hook' boys into learning and keep them 'hooked' – motivated and concentrating. Here's a list summarising what you can do:

- Give appropriate praise.
- Value boys for what they do well.
- Make clear how to succeed, and make success achievable.
- Tell boys that you admire and value them.
- Help boys to develop the language of emotion.
- Use humour.
- Set up learning circles.
- Provide scripts to help develop verbal communication.
- Define quality communication.
- Use non-verbal communication.
- Develop collaborative groupwork/teamwork.
- Assume that boys want to read fiction.
- Use boys' desire for order and hierarchy to teach reading in an explicit, structured way.

- Always keep in mind boys' greater tendency to reading disorders such as dyslexia.
- Model good reading.
- Use writing frames.
- Use 2, 3, 5, 1.
- Consider single-gender teaching.
- Give clear instructions.
- Plan for levels of escalation.
- Rehearse behaviour-management scripts.
- Diffuse volatile situations with humour.
- Protect pride.
- Deliver bite-sized learning.

And the most important of all:
- Raise your expectations of boys.

Chapter 9
I want to establish boy-friendly teaching

Boy-friendly classrooms

This part of the chapter takes the form of a case study written by a very talented teacher with whom I've been working and learning. His name is Ian Tompkins and he is a lead practitioner at Redwell Junior School in Northampton.

Case study

The practical features of a boy-friendly classroom

The classroom ethos can have a profound effect on learning. If it is not positive, learning will be hindered. However, if you manage to match it to the needs of the children, progress will be enhanced.

By carefully observing the needs of my Year-3 pupils, nineteen of whom were boys, I devised a learning environment that catered for their needs. I believe that having a boy-friendly classroom encourages the boys without disadvantaging the girls, and I've monitored the effects through ongoing assessment.

I believe that many children, especially boys, thrive on competition. They display a willingness to better themselves, and through peer involvement feel as if they belong to a team. By supporting a team ethic, children learn behaviour associated with life skills, a key part of the DfES Social and Emotional Aspects of Learning (SEAL) programme. This was why I used the idea of house teams. I displayed a league table at the front of the classroom that included five names of football teams from the premiership. Each child was allocated to a team and could earn points for their group in all areas of school life, not just the academic part.

I want children that I teach to become responsible, co-operative, life-long learners. To help with this I feel it's important that they have the opportunity to work alongside a wide range of their peers during the course of the week. I introduced home and away seats as a means to promote this. This meant that the children had different seats depending on the focus of the particular lesson. Home seats were grouped by ability for targeted work, enabling effective differentiation. Away seats were for mixed-ability groups, enabling more flexible partnerships – including mixed-gender pairings and opportunities for peer support and peer evaluation. The children became used to these ways of working very quickly.

After a while, I introduced European seats, which enable the children to choose whom they sit next to. I use these seats for art, design and technology, and music. I found that when the boys work with friends of their own choice they work with enthusiasm, producing a better quality of result.

When it comes to teaching and learning I always think about the success criteria – what the children need to know in order to succeed. I share this with the children at the beginning of each lesson, alongside the learning objective. This way there are fewer chances of failure.

I found that many of the boys in my class had difficulty concentrating for sustained periods of time. I decided to divide my lessons into manageable chunks that were accompanied by reminders of where we were heading and where we had come from. Pace is an important way to prevent boys from being distracted, so once the learning objective and success criteria had been shared, I decided to keep the first chunk of my lesson to ten minutes or less.

I use mini-whiteboards a great deal in my lessons. I think they are a fantastic resource that allow children to display answers to directed questions or tasks instantly and encourage focused paired discussion. I differentiate using these boards, asking some groups to supply the answer, while others need to show their reasoning too. I call this pair–share work.

I found that it was important to continue to break the time up once the children were working independently. I did this by giving targets for what they should have done by when, linked to their ability. I tended to allow ten to fifteen minutes to pass before stopping the class to have a brain break, enabling them to do something active in their seats to recharge their batteries and refocus. A short exercise routine is a useful brain break.

After a review of the learning objective and success criteria, the children worked for another ten to fifteen minutes before sharing their work in pairs. Each child evaluated their partner's work using a 'sandwich' technique – a positive comment, followed by an area for improvement, followed by another positive comment. This may involve verbal or written feedback. The remainder of the lesson gave the children an opportunity to act upon the advice given to them by their partner before a plenary.

I found that this approach had a positive impact on the learning of all the children in my class, with the boys showing a great desire to succeed. I maintained the interest levels of the boys by keeping the different parts of lessons short and simple in an ethos of value and trust. In fact, that would form the basis of one of my tips about boy-friendly teaching and learning. The others are as follows:

- From the outset, find out what interests the boys in your group and use it to everyone's advantage.
- Ask boys what aspects of learning they enjoy and listen to their replies.
- Break lessons into manageable parts, and include a focus on a range of learning styles.
- Give boys the opportunity to express themselves by sharing and evaluating their work.
- Include brain breaks, mini-reviews, pair–share work, self- and peer-evaluation.
- Most importantly, provide a framework so that boys know what is expected of them in the next part of a lesson.
- Experiment with seating arrangements so that you give children opportunities to work with others of similar and different abilities.
- Provide healthy competition and recognition for achievements associated with life skills.
- Use positive praise as frequently as you can.
- Take calculated risks.

Becoming a boy-friendly teacher

Ian's case study demonstrates how easy it can be to give a classroom a boy-friendly ethos. I like his use of football vocabulary to name and manage groupwork, and the way he engages boys with assessment for learning.

When I visited him we worked together on developing the effectiveness of this second aspect in his classroom. He knew he was using appropriate techniques, but remained unconvinced of their impact on his boys' learning, so we did a little mirror coaching as a way to develop him into an even more effective boy-friendly teacher.

Lynne: Fantastic! I used a very similar approach with my class of twenty boys and ten girls. If you have not had a wide gender split before, some of these ideas may seem risky. Build up your learning community and talk to the kids about the risk. They are likely to enjoy these new ways of learning and will want to help them be successful.

Jo: Using what boys enjoy doing and integrating this into the classroom makes perfect sense. My sons love to play football, but the only time I have seen aspects of it used is when boys are given yellow or red cards for poor behaviour.

Arthur: Sometimes we get to sit in different seats like at Golden Time and when we're not working, like when we're doing puzzles or reading.

Mirror coaching is an effective way to develop teaching skills. It puts the person being coached in full control of setting their own professional development targets and success criteria for up to six lesson observations and feedback sessions. The coach's role is therefore somewhat different from an inspector's, or even an adviser's. Consequently, the mirror coach needs to have these qualities:

- Non-judgemental and open-minded – there is no official standard against which lessons are observed. The coach records what happens for the purposes of analysis in the feedback session.
- Trustworthy – no aspect of the coaching is passed on unless the teacher gives their permission. The teacher 'owns' all the evidence collected.
- Collaborative – coach and teacher work together for the sole purpose of enriching the teacher's teaching and the pupils' learning.
- Able to hold back giving advice – the teacher draws their own conclusions about how they can best enrich their practice by reflecting on the evidence collected by the coach and being guided by their open questions.

In addition, an effective coach needs to be:

- an attentive listener;
- a perceptive questioner;
- a thorough observer;
- a careful recorder of events;
- an experienced teacher.

In a key period of our work together, Ian asked me to look at his use of assessment for learning. He wanted to know whether his use of it was helping the boys in his class. He asked me to collect video evidence during a PE lesson concerned with developing symmetrical sequences. We decided that I would concentrate on the work of two lower-achieving boys. During the lesson, I collected several short video clips that showed them:

- creating their sequence
- rehearsing the sequence
- self-assessing their work
- being assessed by another pair – two girls
- adapting their sequence in the light of this assessment.

During our feedback session, Ian concluded that the boys were able to respond accurately to positive suggestions from their peers. What he decided to do next was, I thought, a master stroke. With the boys' permission, he showed the video clips to the rest of the class and asked them to assess their own peer assessment. This proved a great idea and one I recommend you try.

Coaching is one of the most effective ways to learn and grow. It will help you to grow professionally, but what should you grow into? Boys are clear about whom they want teaching them. They want teachers who:

- are warm, yet firm
- listen to and value them
- give them responsibility

- let them take risks
- let them explore, experiment and argue
- teach them using real objects, visits and artefacts
- respond to their suggestions
- have a sense of humour
- expect them to do well
- don't make assumptions about what they already know.

With acknowledgment for list items to Steve Biddulph, Gary Wilson and the Literacy Trust.

Boy-friendly lessons

On page 63 is a planning guide designed to help you bring together some of the ideas from this section in a manageable way. Photocopy it to have beside you as an aide-mémoire when you are planning your lessons and schemes of work.

Boy-friendly profiles

Finally, there is a template on page 64 to help guide you through thinking about the challenges of teaching boys and how you can best respond to them. It will take some time to build up a full picture of each boy you work with. The quality of help you will be able to give will be in direct relation to the depth of your understanding.

Conclusion

Over the foregoing pages we've learned about what makes boys tick, what motivates them, and how this knowledge can be used to teach them effectively. Many teachers struggle with their boys for two reasons:

1. They don't understand them and their behaviour.
2. The current educational system is not boy friendly and is only slowly responding to boys' needs.

From the outset I proposed that there isn't really a problem with boys and their achievement. The problem lies in what we assess and how we assess it. Assessment is girl friendly and prevents the boys from showing what they do best. However, we must also remember that each boy is an individual and many do not fit that cheeky, boisterous, roguish stereotype. The ideas I presented for thinking about boys in this book can be applied equally well to girls and to adult learners.

We looked at boys through six lenses:
- brain
- values
- family
- school
- society
- culture

We developed a rounded picture of who they are and how they behave. I proposed that this greater understanding leads to enriched teaching and learning for boys, and that better teaching for boys is also better for girls.

Section II presented many ideas for developing teaching by looking at how to play to boys' strengths and how to support their weaknesses. Brain-friendly learning and environments were considered alongside emotional intelligence, literacy and learning styles.

I hope that you've been able to develop your work with boys further, whether as a class teacher, school leader, consultant or adviser. Please take what you want from the book and adapt it to your own circumstances. No single book can hope to cover all aspects of boys' learning and I'm sure you've developed effective ideas of your own. You are, after all, a creative professional. You are in the business of creating professional educational solutions for your learners.

It would be wonderful if this conclusion were not seen as an end but a beginning. The combined talents and experience of each person who reads this sentence would be extraordinary. If each of you shared just one of your successes or ideas for teaching boys, we'd have a terrific free resource. To facilitate this, I've created an area of my website for boys' achievement: www.thinkingclassroom.co.uk/boys. Go visit!

Thanks for reading. I hope I've helped you in your work and learning.

Resources

Other books by Mike Fleetham

How to Create and Develop a Thinking Classroom. LDA: Cambridge. 2003
Multiple Intelligences in Practice. Network Continuum: London. 2006
Pocket Pal: Multiple Intelligences. Network Continuum: London. 2007
Thinking Stories to Wake up Your Mind. LDA: Cambridge. 2007
Fleetham, M. and P. Harris-Burland. *Daily Brainteasers 7–9.* Scholastic: London. 2005
Fleetham, M. and L. Measor. *Moving to Secondary School.* Network Continuum: London. 2005

References

Addy, L. (2003) *How to Understand and Support Children with Dyspraxia.* LDA: Cambridge

Attwood, T. (1998) *Asperger's Syndrome: A Guide for Parents and Professionals.* Jessica Kingsley: London

Biddulph, S. (2003) *Raising Boys.* HarperCollins: London

Blythman, J. (2000) *The Food our Children Eat.* Fourth Estate: London

Davidson, R. and S. Vine (2007) *The Great Big Glorious Book for Girls.* Viking: London

Enright, D. and G. MacDonald (2006) *The Boys' Book: How to Be the Best at Everything.* Buster Books: London

Foster, J. (2007) *The Girls' Book: How to Be the Best at Everything.* Buster Books: London

Gurian, M. and K. Stevens (2007) *The Minds of Boys.* Wiley: Chichester

Haddon, M. (2004) *The Curious Incident of the Dog in the Night Time.* Vintage: London

Hallowell, C. (1987) *Father to the Man.* Morrow: New York

Iggulden, C. and H. Iggulden (2006) *The Dangerous Book for Boys.* HarperCollins: London

McIlvain, A. (2007) 'What Do Boys Really Think?' *Junior Education*, February

Neanon, C. (2002) *How to Identify and Support Children with Dyslexia.* LDA: Cambridge

O'Regan, F. (2002) *How to Teach and Manage Children with ADHD.* LDA: Cambridge

Portwood, M. (2007) *Developmental Dyspraxia: Identification and Intervention: A Manual for Parents and Professionals.* David Fulton: London

Prashnig, B. (2006) *Pocket PAL: Learning Styles and Personalized Teaching.* Network Continuum: London

Sherratt, D. (2005) *How to Support and Teach Children on the Autism Spectrum.* LDA: Cambridge

Whiting, M. (2003) *Dump the Junk.* Moonscape

Build-a-boy template

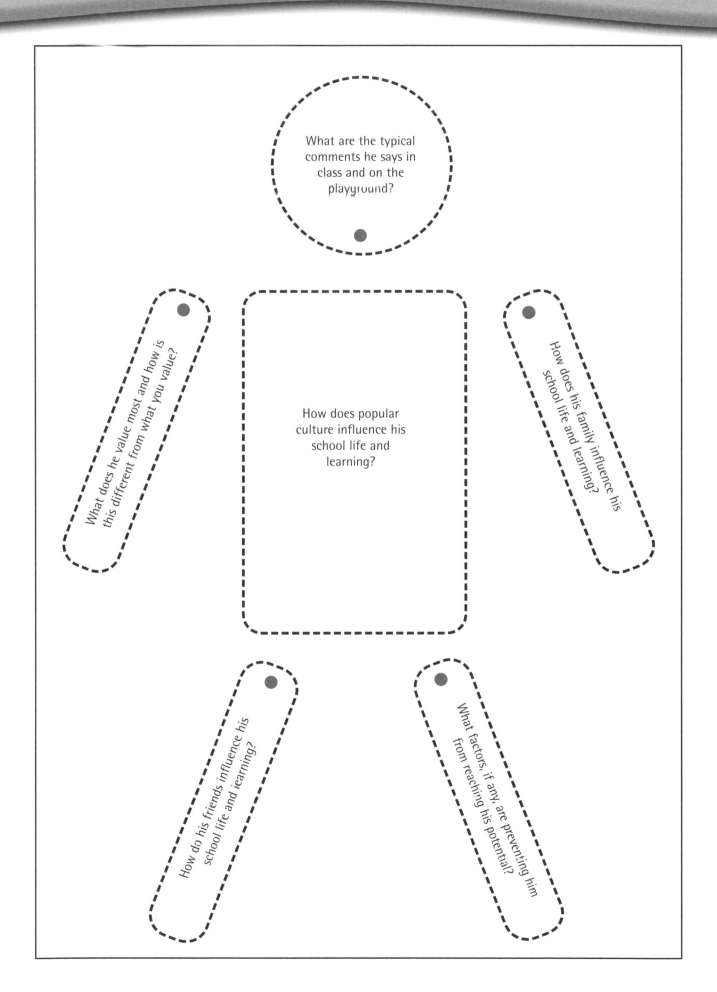

What are the typical comments he says in class and on the playground?

What does he value most and how is this different from what you value?

How does his family influence his school life and learning?

How does popular culture influence his school life and learning?

How do his friends influence his school life and learning?

What factors, if any, are preventing him from reaching his potential?

Children's television

For each show listed below, put a tick in the column that is closest to your answer – only one tick per show.

TV Show	Never heard of it	Heard of it, but not seen it	Watched it one or more times	Watch it regularly
Bamzooki				
Basil Brush				
Batman				
Blue Peter				
Camp Lazlo				
Ed, Edd and Eddy				
Fairly Odd Parents				
Foster's Home for Imaginary Friends				
Gina's Laughing Gear				
Kim Possible				
My Gym Partner's a Monkey				
My Parents are Aliens				
Pokemon				
Powerpuff Girls				
Prank Patrol				
Raven				
Samurai Jack				
Scooby Doo				
The Slammer				
SpongeBob SquarePants				
Suite Life				
Tracey Beaker				
Totals				
Multiply score by	0	1	2	3
New totals				
Overall total (add the four above)				

An overall score of 0 probably means that you don't have a TV and never have had.

The maximum score of 66 may well indicate that you have too much free time on your hands.

A low score may indicate that you need to be more aware of the influences that are commonplace to many children, especially boys, in your group.

With boys in mind

Top planning tips for teaching boys well

When organising learning:

- pair girls with boys during listening tasks
- plan for regular breaks during an activity
- let boys tell each other what they've learned
- provide risk and competition
- provide clear success criteria with reasons
- take physical brain breaks
- partition learning into ten-minute blocks
- use competitive learning teams
- use team roles
- call lessons challenges

Learning activities

Plan for the following activities to appear regularly in your lessons:

- pre-bulleted lists
- emotional recipes
- learning circles
- scripts
- quality communication
- non-verbal communication
- writing frames
- 2, 3, 5, 1

Use multiple intelligences, especially the following:

Intelligence
What a boy will want to do

Bodily/Kinaesthetic
Move, touch, handle, build, make, construct

Mathematical/Logical
Think, ask questions, seek order, have reasons, know the learning objective and lesson format

Visual/Spatial
Watch, imagine, create, visualise, paint, draw, watch television, look at photographs, read graphic novels

Intrapersonal
Be independent, work alone, have their own space, set and monitor their own targets

Boy-friendly profile

Name:	DoB:	Class:	Teacher:

What might be preventing him from achieving his best?

How might the following be affecting his learning?

Brain	
Values	
Family	
School	
Society	
Culture	

Things he typically says:

His learning style preferences:

Prefers	Tick	Prefers	Tick
Watching		Cold classroom	
Listening		Bright classroom	
Talking		Dim classroom	
Reading		Taking regular breaks	
Touching		Working with others	
Moving around		Background noise/music	
Silence		Warm classroom	
Working alone		Afternoons	
Mornings		Frequent snacks/drinks	

His intelligences/strengths with examples:

Musical/Rhythmic – He can . . .
Verbal/Linguistic – He can . . .
Existential – He can . . .
Interpersonal – He can . . .
Intrapersonal – He can . . .
Visual/Spatial – He can . . .
Mathematical/Logical – He can . . .
Bodily/Kinaesthetic – He can . . .

Things he may be thinking:

How we can help:

Teacher	
Assistant	
School	
Family	